MADE IN CANADA

Edited by Douglas Lochhead & Raymond Souster

New Poems of the Seventies

"Projected Slide of an Unknown Soldier"
and "Carrying Food Home in Winter"
by Margaret Atwood
and "Another Space," "Knitter's Prayer,"
"Fly: On Webs" and "A Backwards Journey"
by P. K. Page
are reprinted by permission of
the Modern Poetry Association.

Reprinted 1971, 1972, 1973

Library of Congress Catalogue Card No. 70–122318
ISBN 0 88750 022 6 (hardcover)
ISBN 0 88750 023 4 (softcover)

Book design by Michael Macklem

Published in Canada by Oberon Press
with the aid of the Canada Council

Printed and bound in England
by Hazell Watson and Viney Ltd.

This anthology is contemporary and has the word "now" stamped all over it. The title was selected with care—*Made in Canada*. It means exactly what it says, and it implies, as we intend it to, that these poems are for export as well as for home consumption. They are meant to be read alongside poems from other countries. This is no bid for instant greatness on the world stage. But it is time for readers to consider the merits of many of the poems here, not because they are Canadian but because they are worthy of comparison with the best poetry being written today in the English-speaking world.

And we go one step further. We believe the sixty-four poets included in *Made in Canada* provide sixty-four reasons for concluding that the poetry scene in English Canada as we enter the Seventies is equalled in variety, excitement and technical excellence only in the United States.

How was the anthology compiled? Some ninety poets were invited to submit poems of their own choosing. The only stipulation we made was that poems submitted should not previously have appeared in book form. We made no attempt to cater to the young or to the old, but tried simply to collect the best and most representative poetry now being written in this country. About sixty poets emerged with work to publish. Our selection represents what we feel is the cream of their submissions. As such it provides a wide enough cross-section of contemporary poetry to make it possible for us to offer a few judgments of our own for what they are worth.

The first and most obvious comment that comes to mind is that in Canada, as in England and the United States, poetry has entered a period of consolidation. This has been noticeable for three or four years, and it is a trend that will probably continue for some time to come. It's not a very surprising state of affairs if we take into account the great strides made in the ten years from 1955 to 1965. Small wonder that the poets have welcomed the chance to catch their collective breath, to regroup their forces, to plan new strategies. The second comment is that very few modern Canadian poets now make any use whatever of either rhyme or regular verse patterns. We have abandoned these traditional devices even more completely than the Americans. Perhaps the experience of the Fifties, when a serious attempt was made to turn the clock back, has stuck in our craw longer than it should. After all, both rhyme and regular verse forms can, if skilfully used, add to such a poem as David Knight's "Military Governors" or John Newlove's "Man Drift." It is fair to say that much of the freedom from form that we have gained in recent years has not been used wisely or well; many poets have forgotten that verse must still sing or it is as good as dead from the moment it appears on the printed page.

Influences are always interesting, if not too revealing. Canadian poetry now draws most of these from south of the 49th parallel. Even if we wanted to fight this tendency, which would be plain silly, we can't turn to England any longer—the poets there are seeking new influences even more desperately than we are. Another source, comparatively untapped as yet, is the best of poetry in other languages—represented by figures like Montale, Vallejo, Enzensberger, Holub, Herbert—to name only the five who come most readily to mind.

But to get down to the poetry at hand, the work exhibited in these pages. What poets are leading the way? Which can be said to have found their own distinctive voice? Which show the most promise for the future?

Among the new poets who quickly established reputations in the Sixties are Margaret Atwood, John Newlove and Michael Ondaatje. Margaret

Atwood is an expert with the tautly-etched scene where more often than not the actors are shadows, where the landscape assumes greater importance than the actors. Her poems move well; the lines are pared down to make every word count. Some critics have complained that her work has a certain coldness. They would prefer her to project more strongly into the real world. But none deny the power of her vision, her sure technique.

John Newlove, if his poems in this collection are any indication, seems to be moving from largely local concerns toward a more inward, personal landscape. A poem such as "Dream" is a good example of this, and incidentally, the use of the prose-poem form suits him very well. Michael Ondaatje, originally from Ceylon, has become known for such luxuriously-appointed poems as "Notes for the legend of Salad Woman," but he too is moving around, not content with past forms and attitudes, as we can see from the very spare, the almost stark directness of "Kim, at half an inch" and "Gold and black."

At the other end of the scale we have Nelson Ball, Paul Dutton, Bill Howell and Henry Weinfield, all four making their first appearance in a Canadian anthology, and all but Nelson Ball relatively unknown. Ball, at twenty-eight the oldest of the group, has drawn his influences unmistakably from recent American models, but has such an individual turn of mind that whatever emerges is very much Canadian and very much his own. Sometimes you imagine him to be a W. W. E. Ross reborn. There is that same sharp eye for natural things, that desire to say much in little, the same joy in looking at the world. Paul Dutton is half the young romantic, half the very solid modern cat as in "Jazz Musician." Bill Howell is from Nova Scotia, an accomplished poet and prose stylist at twenty-four. Look how he gives a new twist to what could be a very pedestrian utterance in "The Long and the Short" and "Mechanics of Living" and how in "The Handle of Tomorrow" he can explore his province's history in a creative, living way. Henry Weinfield, at twenty-one the youngest poet in the book, is the least "open" of the four, writing a poetry of the intellect which in some strange way involves the reader, even though its meanings are always carefully shrouded.

A number of poets, older than these, have been working away at their craft for a number of years, but for one reason or another haven't yet achieved any widespread prominence. Tom Arnett is one of these. While best known as an organizer and teacher at the Toronto New Writers' Workshop, he is a proficient poet in his own right whose chief interest at the moment is in mixed media. Take "In Memoriam," a tribute to another Toronto poet who was largely neglected in his lifetime: how many poets could say so much in so few words? Then there is Genevieve Bartole, wife of Kenneth McRobbie, whose work has been growing in strength these past few years; she too has not been published except in the magazines. Bill Bissett, to some the *enfant terrible* of Canadian verse, has published a large body of work, much of it of uneven quality, but still experimentally alive, full of the turmoil of living and charged with the vitality of the West-Coast scene.

Ralph Cunningham, still almost unknown as a Canadian poet, shows in his "Rockabye for Benny" and "Chinese" a preoccupation with the unusual phrase, the strange metaphor, the audacious simile. His close friend, George Whipple, also largely unknown, exhibits many of the same concerns, and in addition has stretched back the boundaries of musical effects that can be achieved with the printed word. For David Donnell, on the other hand, intellect and imagination go hand in hand. He has come a long way since his first volume of a few years ago. Patrick Lane, by way of contrast, is content to paint the back country of Western Canada he knows so well, and does it in a loving, immediate manner. Dorothy Roberts, a niece of Sir Charles G. D. Roberts, has the same sure eye for landscape as her uncle and handles the longer line with quiet authority. Finally, from among the established poets who seem to be writing today with fresh energy and direction, one cannot help but single out Earle Birney, R. G. Everson, Ralph Gustafson (his "Nocturne: Prague 1968" will be for many the most memorable poem in the book) and Dorothy Livesay.

Earlier we said that we find promise in this collection. The promise shows in the wide range of subjects—from giblets to fireflies, from military governors to swamps, from a waiter's smile to a carnival cantata. Canadian poetry as it enters the Seventies still shows the influence of contemporary American writing. But this kind of cross-fertilization has been going on for many years and the influence is a healthy one.

Made in Canada is more than a sampler. It is a cut through the Canadian fabric. It shows what is going on in English-Canadian poetry as we enter the Seventies. The Sixties proved an exciting time for poetry in this country. Much pioneer work was done, especially in freeing verse forms and developing a feeling for new forms to fit the new content. There still remains the challenge for all poets to make the next moves and to consolidate or reject the gains of the past.

Made in Canada is, we believe, the one anthology now available that charts the new dimensions and points to the areas where poetic promise is still to be fulfilled. The wonder is that we have come so far is so short a time.

DOUGLAS LOCHHEAD/RAYMOND SOUSTER

Milton Acorn

I sold those tools because the carpenter trade was too hard on my nerves. Not the trade, which I loved, but the conditions in the trade. I fully intended to go on working and I did for a while. It was Al Purdy who now forgets he was the one who originally urged me to devote all my time to writing. A writer who tries to work part-time and write part-time is thrown precisely into those areas of exploitation where the wrong sort of blink of an eyelid, or a nosebleed, can be reasons for getting fired. About my poems: what I have been

She . . .

The frame's of ebony, it is a door
, a place to look where she pre-empts the spaces
because her hair, because she is
as waves in those spaces. . . .
Nothing about her is quiet, no more than the moon
on a night of meteors. . . .

You look into the frame as into a mirror gone
wrong,
thinking that she isn't you—
steps
are
in
the frame
; and you look for the scuffed shadows of her feet
where she may have stepped, may step, may never
step:
You have your thoughts and hers are a reflection
as yours are a reflection;
hers could be yours
and yours could be hers;
and how do they swirl in her brain now
as if they were yours?

Thinking of the frame as a door, the door as a
frame
and you
in the room as a frame, the frame as a room
; the identity of I and you
—her dress steps into the eye as you—thinking
of clouds moving across her eyes, as you;
and there are motes of life
cells struggling through her eyes
like you
: thinking of this, and her, you are
words yourself—a sentence dropped half-way
through
and thought of—

told is that I am writing merely what the other writers only dare to think. I'll buy that—but when are they going to do something about their thoughts? Besides, as works of literary craftsmanship, my poems are superb. Who said that? I said that. The message of my poems? It is not a liberal one. It is that exploitation is going to stop. It is going to stop because it is going to be stopped. That means each individual exploiter is going to be stopped. For those exploiters who are reading this I will clarify further by saying you, you, you—and especially YOU, you son of a bitch, are going to be stopped.

A sentence that is me; a sentence I complete and
think you said
; a sentence answering itself
while the tongue hangs as a cloud
and in her mindseye moves as a cloud, and you

Of souls the most near
are
the most mysterious. . . .
Nothing so mysterious as her presence
in herself, and with you
as a term of her spaces. . . .

Ode to the Timothy Eaton Memorial Church

You get up on that cross / This time brother. . . .
A carpenter, you say, gave up His life for you
And another carpenter knocked together
Two stout sticks. . . .
How charming were the Proletarians of Old
Times!
I'm afraid us modern crew can't manage
That kind of mental weather;
If what you cross your hearts with crossed fingers
To say is true

To save your souls?
How quaint? Take me for instance
—I'd like to stand in for the Devil on his day off:
How I'd stoke!
Or
To make a better image

With what gusto I'd stand on the podium / And
wield my baton
To direct the instruments manned by the fiends of
Hell—
Moans! Screams! Choked prayers and sincere
curses! What cacophony!
Don't twitch!
Here's your crown of thorns Sir!
Bravely bear the royal pricks! You know
You were right—
That vision of a decent Man
A Good God even
Bearing all sorts of pains for the sake of sinners,
Or to put it more bluntly—the rich;
Does give a certain satisfaction
I'd say a certain peace to the spirit
As long as a few amendments are made
Like, You, the guilty
Suffering instead of the innocent. . .
Much as you lust for a pure paschal lamb;
Paschal snakes are much more satisfactory
To me. . . .
That's right!
Don't be shy!
Lick off that bloody sweat!
In such a circumstance the tongue's better than
Kleenex,
Like candy on an exasperating day:
And while you're tasting that Savour—My small
mercy
—ponder on what your lying legend of a
Voluntarily
Suffering Christ really means.

Live with Me on Earth

Live with me on Earth among red berries and the
  bluebirds
And leafy young twigs whispering
Within such little spaces, between such floors of
  green, such figures in the clouds
That two of us could fill our lives with delicate
  wanting:

Where stars past the spruce copse mingle with
  fireflies
Or the dayscape flings a thousand tones of light
  back at the sun—
Be any one of the colours of an Earth lover;
Walk with me and sometimes cover your shadow
  with mine.

Live with me on Earth under the invisible daylight
  Moon;
Where the pages of a book by Irving Layton
Or any other author who has forgotten
Snap fluttering, unlike a butterfly tethered with
  a thread:

Where a word, a sentence, a philosophy
Expends and regathers itself; as a nude athlete
Flings his fatigued body
Onto the grassy bank in a hollow while the
  crowd's yell grows dim—

And if this or that one does not rise, someone will
  rise
When a thought leaps and skips like the recorded
  note of a bugle
Stored and then replayed, leaps and skips
Gathering newness from each listener.

George Amabile (born 1936) has published widely in Canada and the States and has appeared in *Prism*, *Quarry*, *The Young American Poets*, *Canadian Forum*, *Canadian Dimension*, *Pluck*, *The New Yorker*, *The New Orleans Review* and *The New Mexico Quarterly*. He co-edits *The Far Point*.

George Amabile

Herr Poetaster Takes a Midnight Snack

What next?
Anger fades like white
knuckles relaxed.

I have overtaxed
my night
life. Drugs, booze & sex.

If I sleep I'll wake to the bright
voices & blades of 9 AM, specks
of dust dancing, children, hindsight.

Having already devoured the slight
shiny wings, he starts on the neck,
then the marrow packed with unscheduled flight.

Fireflies

The Milky Way bleeds
a trace of cloud.
Up close, the violence
of asteroids
disintegrating lights.

On the distant prairie
a slim hovering wash:
a city, the streetlights . . .

The windshield aglow with wreckage.

Pale scar in the rear-view mirror.

Up in Smoke

July 4th. Shot
like a mortar trailing sparks
it's lost to sight. *Pock:*
tall curdled feathers

pink or chalky green,
a voodoo headdress
out of the oohs & ahs.
Also, Disney stardust

showers, pinwheels, the shock
& puff of simple flak.
Again and again bunched
memorial smoke wilts

to slight fire, soot,
and there at the end, in the centre
of the High School football field
just off the ground, *Old*

Glory hisses & glares—
five minutes of colourful holocaust
spent like jet fuel.
The crowd melts, leaving

popcorn, empty bottles, cigarette
butts. Scrappy flames
break out in the ashes, light up
the frayed threads of smoke

the grid-work underneath,
a thought-out plan, a city.
Lost in this flickering rubble
I can almost hear

the occasional faded scream.
Hanoi, London, Rome. . . .

I was born in Winnipeg in 1935. I am a writer by trade and an idler by inclination. My published writing ranges from history books to satirical revue. At the moment I am working on a feature film, a musical for radio, an educational television show and a novel.

In Memoriam: Pádraig Ó Broin

Pádraig is dead,
that meek, little man of the towering personality.

"People must know how to dispense death when
it is the only cure,"
he would say.

But he wept
when that cocky, little black dog died.

The Pro

Tom Arnett

There's a cold snake in my bed,
who mechanically feeds me sawdust
until my buddha belly,
gorged by smooth-as-automatic-transmission ritual,
contemplates its own swollen starvation.

This much practised pro, with its super-mystic
motions,
expects to satisfy me in less time than it takes
to repack a super-personality in its little, black bag.
But I'm left so full of plastic soup
that my heart drowns in my gut!

Who called prostitution "the world's oldest
profession"?
The first pro is this sanctimonious soul-saver
whose silky sermon persuades
both Eve and me to feed on wax apples.

National Film Board: Shorts Before Features

Born 1939. Three books of poetry: *The Circle Game* (1966), *The Animals in that Country* (1968) and *The Journals of Susanna Moodie* (1970). One novel: *The Edible Woman* (1969). Governor General's Award for Poetry in 1966.

Margaret Atwood

Later we will have stories about people,
faces closeup and
bodies, loving or shooting

but first we have a word
in code from a separate country:

The sun was not always there
or warm enough

but now the ice is changing
to real water

over the pebbles and sand
mosses move in

short waxy flowers
with tough leaves come up and out

too fast; life coats
the ground thinly.

A rodent is killed by a hook-
beaked bird

other birds gather
on the beach. The sun dwindles

shaggy hoofed animals
turn to the wind and

in shades of white
which descend layer on layer
winter ends all.

Cyclops

You, going along the path,
mosquito-doped, with no moon, the flashlight
a single orange eye

unable to see what is beyond
the capsule of your dim
sight, what shape

contracts to a heart
with terror, bumps
among the leaves, what makes
a bristling noise like a fur throat.

Is it true you do not wish to hurt them?

Is it true you have no fear?
Take off your shoes then,
let your eyes go bare,
swim in their darkness as in a river

do not disguise
yourself in armour.

They watch you from hiding:
you are a chemical
smell, a cold fire, you are
giant and indefinable

In their monstrous night
thick with possible claws
where danger is not knowing,

you are the hugest monster.

Projected Slide of an Unknown Soldier

Upon the wall a face
uttered itself
in light, pushing
aside the wall's darkness;

Around it leaves, glossy,
perhaps tropical, not making
explicit whether the face was
breaking through them, wore them
as disguise, was crowned
with them or sent them
forth as rays,
a slippery halo;

The clothes were invisible,
the eyes
hidden; the nose
foreshortened: a muzzle.
Hair on the upper lip.
On the skin the light shone, wet
with heat; the teeth
of the open mouth reflected it
as absolute.

The mouth was open
stretched wide in a call or howl
(there was no tongue)
of agony, ultimate
command or simple famine.
The canine teeth ranged back
into the throat and vanished.

The mouth was filled with darkness.
The darkness in the open mouth
uttered itself, pushing
aside the light.

Carrying Food Home in Winter

I walk uphill through the snow
hard going
brown paper bag of groceries
balanced low on my stomach,
heavy, my arms stretching
to hold it turn all tendon.

Do we need this paper bag
my love, do we need this bulk
of peels and cores, do we need
these bottles, these roots
and bits of cardboard
to keep us floating
as on a raft
above the snow I sink through?

The skin creates
islands of warmth
in winter, in summer
islands of coolness.

The mouth performs
a similar deception.

I say I will transform
this egg into a muscle
this bottle into an act of love

This onion will become a motion
this grapefruit
will become a thought.

Nelson Ball

I was born in Clinton, Ont. in 1942. Studied at the University or Waterloo. Own and operate Weed/Flower Press. My own books are *Room of Clocks* (1965), *Beaufort's Scale* (1967) and *Sparrows* (1968).

Arrangement in a Vase

It is not a forest, although
it has that appearance.

It is plural—
a bunch of dried grasses.

You might find them
in autumn, clumped

about a fence post. They
were picked singularly

and in this warm room
their appearance is singular.

Location

We drive north past a red barn.
Our direction presses it south.

A stone house passes from behind it.
The house and barn have their place

as does a tree that grows between them.
The tree takes what it can

from the earth and air.
Our presence is elemental.

Winter Poem

What is left that
isn't dead?

The eyes move.

Let in fresh air!

I re-read William's poem
because I depend

upon the red wheelbarrow.
Heavy snow boots today.

Place the hands
on a surface—

your skin—
warm and alive.

The Affluent Society

The neon signs promise.
Promise "everything."

Nothing is received. We burn out
like the missing letters.

The signs will be repaired.
We will be replaced.

Fingers

The space I don't fill not placing
my fingers between yours.

Born Winnipeg, 1940. Now teaching at the University of Alberta in Edmonton. A former editor of *Quarry*. Poems and reviews have appeared in *Canadian Forum*, *Canadian Literature*, *Dalhousie Review*, *Fiddlehead*, *Open Letter*, *Prism*, *Quarry* and *Queen's Quarterly*.

Douglas Barbour

"she" as foreground in portrait of a boy

Only long before he
ever dreamed or
lay among the apples

we know very well that she
was planning small disasters
and waiting

where he never tossed
nor turned nor
threw his sheets in crumples

on the floor and fell
with the cinnamon earth
to trying bites of the apples

nor wandered in tall
grass nor wondered
at the bright sky

that yawned above
and screamed sound-
lessly that day

she found him where
he accidentally tripped
over adolescence:

it was never the same
again.

a small song

These few things
of which I have some knowledge,
This life
through which I walk:

It is dark and
I want to dance: don't
dare. The land
folds over, stones
rattle on the bleak
distances.

poem for someone else

I have not my own pain
to write from, nor
do I stand as you
do, at the gates, foolishly staring
over my shoulder
at the small figure fading in mist.

Oh, I have felt it, some
times, like a knife slicing
slivers of skin under the nail,

but not for long. You

almost revel in it, a continuous
low-intensity burning
leading to song. Which is

good as far as it goes.

I praise your song, friend, it is
good. But not the pain.
Do not believe the pain
is necessity. It is
only an occasion
for a possible song.

Genevieve Bartole

I was born in Saskatchewan in 1927 and lived there until I went to Columbia University. Later I worked in libraries in Toronto and London, England. I am now married to Kenneth McRobbie and live in Winnipeg. My poems have appeared in *Canadian Forum*, *Combustion*, *Fiddlehead*, *Galliard* and *Yes*, and have been broadcast by the CBC.

Breakup

Ice lens
of the river
breaking open,
how coldly it regards me!

Frazil over mushweed
where the pickerel lurk.
All winter they have evaded
the rod of the ice fisherman
and light spilled
  through a hole
in their sleep.

Now
the breakup threatens
to let them through
  to the surface.
A far sea roars.

Can the wild goose hear it
  flying over the river?
See it?
And the cat know it
sniffing bird tracks
  in the last snow?

O God, I am not like a cat—
to take into the night
light borrowed from the day.
What I see are shadows in motion,
and of such deep substance,
  white world, bleeding
shadows, dark

As the darkness of water.
Moving nearer its edge I see
a deer of such indescribable beauty

it must surely travel the river forever
embalmed in an ice floe.
Its antlers make its own grey
headstone.

Ice-stitched carcass:
—did only a raven, perhaps
back in the forest
witness the lost footing
the hurtle over the bank?
Only the sun see how life runs
slowly out of the mouth
in freezing?

Till the moon rose
and in your glassy eyeball
reflected again
the grey-green tents of treetops
the moving brunt panorama
of bank and boulder.

Now it is over.
You have come so far. And though
there is mercy tonight
in an east wind
the river's mouth has little taste
for you yet
stuffed as it is with ice
and brown weed water.

Phoenix

Even in my last death
will there be this shadow. There
will be no sun as when
each day was

as a new beginning,
only the warm thin shadow of a girl
monument to youth
   and my death.

It cannot leave
until my sun goes down
   cannot move
until it drinks my blood.
Standing in my footsteps
its body drinks from
   the well of my soul.

There it is—
mother whore or saint
it cannot dance its life perfectly
   without complicity
from my death
would wither through the long night
   under my low ceiling
like a bird caught in a tomb
without my skeletal
cage of mercy.

   If I turned suddenly
would I meet the eyes of my own reflection?
Is it a shadow still, or a bird?
If a bird
will its wings
with my help and blood
be strong enough to fly,
living, into the face
   of another sun?

Born Regina, 1924. Translations of poetry from Swedish, Finnish and Norwegian have appeared in Canadian and American periodicals. Books: *The Wandering World* (1959), *The Unimaginable Circus, Theatre & Zoo* (1965), *Changes* (1968). Contributed to *Poetry 62* and *New Directions Anthology 21* (1969). Now writing a critical study of Northrop Frye.

Ronald Bates

15 February, 1969

St. Valentine's was over
  snow still on the ground
    as usual here
the day, an ordinary sunny day
  a month from the Ides of March
and the usual Saturday things were being done

nobody expected that the air
  would start to smell like flowers

accounts vary according to source
  and imagination
but *The Free Press* non-committally reported
  that a corporation lawyer was the first:

at 12:25 PM
  (a very punctual person, he was on his way
  to lunch at 12:30 at the Iroquois)
smelled the odour of roses
  at the corner of King and Clarence

apparently some minutes later
  a transport driver who was born on a farm
but was stopped at a light on Richmond at Oxford,
      going south
  found his cab filled with the scent of lilacs

soon
  sufferers from hay fever began phoning
  their doctors and out-patients at hospitals
complaining of goldenrod

then the radio stations got the messages
  lines began to jam
with anxious, even hysterical queries
  about the odour of:
  violets

lily of the valley
hyacinth & narcissus
apple blossom & orange & cherry
even honeysuckle

and from the most improbable places
like the tannery by the CPR tracks
or Labatt's

as the afternoon wore on
more and more of the ordinary day
was submerged or transmuted by the perfumed
air
so that absolute strangers in the streets
stopped to compare their olfactory sensations

the flower stalls in the market—
well—
just imagine—
the situation began to assume the state of crisis
which a full-scale two-day blizzard brings about

the traffic superintendent of Police had already
been on radio and TV
five times
calling for action
and the Mayor was about to proclaim. . .

when, suddenly it ended,
all the familiar smells were back:
diesel fumes
automobile exhaust
the tannic acid smell of skin
cigarette smoke
the smell of stale cigars
and all the usual in and outdoor fug

everything, in short, was back to normal

and yet there were a few who knew
that flowers smell like air

Driving East on Cheapside

the distant end of the street
in the rear-vision mirror
holds the sunset like a stain
gory orange and pink
bleeding down the sky
and memory

(the best symbols are always for real)

ends of streets erupting
into prairie or dribbling
off the planks of docks to float
the seaway or disappearing
like shadows among trees

(there are as many ends of streets as days)

the new facades of buildings
hunched to the east
and glazed in amber
take on the strange patina sometimes seen
in the old masters
or remembered from the past
out of a different atmosphere

(certain streets have double-ended time)

I would someday like to walk
right through the sunset
a clown bursting out of
a crepe-paper hoop
laughing in white-face
but with the mouth
and eyes
fixed in wonder
finding
a sun-drenched hollow instead

of the arc-lamp circle and the dead
sawdust smell

(streets and sunsets come together
reminding
us
of what we did
and whether we did it well)

The Thrushes Do Not Die Out

Walter Bauer was born in the Saxon town of Merseburg, Germany, in 1904, the fifth child of a labourer. He took up his first post in a village school in 1928 and in the same year published his first book. In 1933 his books were banned by the Nazi regime. He was drafted in 1940 and forced against his will to serve in the German army. In 1952 he emigrated to Canada to make a fresh start. For a few years he was a packer, dishwasher, labourer. Later he enrolled in the University of Toronto, where he took his degrees and now teaches.

Walter Bauer

I

They have hunted down
The poet.
Yes, they have killed him,
The good-for-nothing, him
Who irritated everybody.
All the nine-to-five men,
All the dutiful housewives—
They have disposed of him.
Yes, like a boy with a slingshot
Who shatters the flight of the thrush
And then, with a shrug,
Kicks
The dead songs into a ditch—
That's how they killed him.
They could not bear his singing
While they slaved
To pay off their mortgages
On the house, on the car,
On their lives.
Yes, they have killed him.
There he lies now in a ditch, now
Their world is exactly
The kind of world they want:
A godforsaken place, good
For making money, good
For growing fat and old without joy.
That's what they wanted, they have no
Regrets at all. They killed him
To get rid of him,
He disturbed them: he wasn't like them.

2

Later a scholar found
A bunch of manuscripts
In the ditch—that is to say
In a miserable room,
And he had them published
With his own assiduous annotations:
He had discovered a dead poet
Ignored by his contemporaries.
There you are, they said,
We always knew there was something
Something quite special in his voice.
Only, why wasn't he like us,
Regular, from nine to five?
He could've made a decent living.
The domestic animals said to the thrush:
Live without wings,
Fly without song.

3

Still later
They put up his statue
And the speaker,
A regular nine-to-five man,
Talked of the eternal
Poet.
Everyone felt elevated.

4

The time came
When no-one any longer paid
Any attention to the statue.
Occasionally a thrush
Would settle on his shoulder
And sing into the dead ear
Of the poet.

5

Later still
A young man discovered
The dead poet's verses
And said, why did I
Not know him? He would've been
My friend,
Yes, he is my friend, I will
Follow in his footsteps, I will
Sing, I will
Not be a nine-to-five man.
Ah, my dead friend, he called,
You have lit up the world for me.

6

Then they started the hunt
All over again.
They will bring him down alright,
Yes, not to worry
They will kill him.
This, they say,
Is no place for thrushes.

7

But the thrushes
Do not die out.

Translated from the German by Henry Beissel

a song for sunsets

goodnite sun
im turning over again
im on the little ball
so slowly rolling
backwards from you

i hope youre there
central & responsible
burning away
all thru the black
of my dumb
somersault

i'll tumble around
& wake to you
the one who never sleeps
never notices
too busy keeping the whole
flock of us
rolling towards vega
without losing
our milky way

goodnite big dad
hasta la vista
hasta luego
we'll switch on now
our own small stars
lie in darkness burning
turning
through unspace untime
& upsadaisy back
i hope to you

Born 1904 in Calgary, then part of the Northwest Territories. Lived around a lot; three childhoods (Prairies, Rockies, B.C. fruit valley), and now entering fourth and last in Vancouver. Current book is *The Poems of Earle Birney* (1969).

Earle Birney

there are delicacies

there are delicacies
  in you
    like the hearts
      of watches
there are filigrees
  without patterns
    and tiny
      locks

i need your help
  to contrive
    keys
theres so little time
  even for the finest
    watches

i think you are a whole city

and yesterday when i first touched
you i started moving
thru one of your suburbs
where all the gardens are fresh
with faces of you
flowering

some girls are only houses
maybe a strip
development
woman you are miles
of boulevards with supple trees
unpruned and full of winding
honesties

so give me time   i want
i want to know
all your squares and cloverleafs
im steering now by a constellation
winking over this nights rim
from some great beachside of you
with highrisers and a spotlit
beaux arts

i can hear your beat-
ing center   will i
will i make it
are there maps of you
i keep circling
imagining
parks fountains your stores

back in my single
bed i wander   your stranger
dreaming i am
your citizen

The Canadian

my who yu born on scorpio sagittarian cusp in 1939 makes me 31 beans divided by 2000 no tomorrows oh lets get together who needs a united front against the enemy lets all 3 billion be untied within we cud

Bill Bissett

start sharin th food thats a gud start 1/2 th world starves since th othr 1/2 aint at all eatin can we skip 1984 please. "The Canadian" was originally publishd in *Awake In Th Red Desert* and in "West of Summer," a compilation of West-Coast poets selected by Al Purdy for *Tamarack Review*.

On the train, back from th Empress
dining car, snowing woodlands
,pulling thru Manitoba, recall
how sum yrs after th second centenary
of th founding of Halifax, which
date I commemorated with sign
above my father's street door,
into two parts i divided, th half
on th left, what once was, before
1749, th Micmac Indian, th second
half, after that time, a British sailor,
on board, telescope to eye, sailing
into harbor, Mountbatten drove by
my father's house that day, part of
th ceremonies, dressed by University gown
& cap, later that year, th woman to be
Queen, then Princess Elizabeth drove
thru Halifax town, in bullet-proof car.

But i was to recall, as i did,
coming back from th dining car, that
sum yrs after Halifax had her bicentenary,
i wrote my third or fourth pome, in
which, constructed as allegory, i did en
vision th society of fact in Canada
as a train, its peopuls classd, & sub-
classed, according to th rank & station,
that is, what they cud claim they owned, or,
who they cud claim owned them, its
peopuls cut off from each other by
such coach cars & compartments.

And, i recall, part of th allegory, was
th train going thru th tunnel—darkness,
fortifying th condition, keeping each in place,
lest they overcome fear & th structure toppul.

It's not such a good allegory, my
friends sd—well, now that sum of my best
friends are in jail—i see its uses,
my boyhood despair—seeing, as th
train rolls thru Manitoba, how it
does seem that still peopul are hungry in
this country, sum of my best friends are
hungry, peopul are hungry, they hunger
for food—outside of this train there is
no food—in it there is good & bad food;
food that will just keep yu strong enuff
to keep yr place—food that is
just good enuff yu dream
of better food—and food that is so good
yu become encouraged to accept
that this train is not going to crash
cannot be changed, from within
or without, is God or Allah's very
handiwork, but where is th food
on this train, this one
to show me Allah in all things,
for then, in ourselves th best food,
we share th bounty
on this Iron Horse.

Sunday Morning

Elizabeth Brewster

Born at Chipman, NB in 1922. Educated at UNB, Radcliffe, the University of Toronto Library School and Indiana University, where I did my doctoral dissertation on George Crabbe. Have worked in libraries in New Brunswick, Ontario and Indiana; at present catalogue rare books at the University of Alberta Library, Edmonton. Books: *East Coast* (1951), *Lillooet* (1954), *Roads* (1957), *Passage of Summer: Selected Poems* (1969).

It is twenty below outside
And something has happened to the church's
heating.
The congregation sits
Heavy-coated,
Huddled in scarves, fur hats,
Hands in pockets.
The man in front of me
Sneezes and shivers.

It is no special day.
Christmas is over,
Lent has not yet started.
It is a long time
To any time.
The priest wears green
For hope.
In January
Green is a cold colour.
His hands look cold.

Luckily, there is no sermon.
The choir sings
Coldly
Rise up, O men of God
And we rise up.

Outdoors the weather is grey.
Snow falls a little,
And a yellow snowplough
Is coming up the street.
A small boy, darting from his mother
And running with arms outstretched
Calls out
"Look at me,
Look at me.

I am a kite
Blowing in the wind."

Northern Sunrise

Drawing my drapes, I see
Pink and purple clouds of dawn
Over the white-roofed city,
Smoke in rising fountains,
The lights of early risers
Twinkling far off,
The new moon, hanging low,
Beginning to pale in the morning sky.

The beautiful northern city
Is a child's Christmas toy
Spread out like blocks
With here and there a tree
Deftly placed,
Discreetly frosted;
And, like a child,
I want to pick it up,
Move a house here, a tree there,
Put more frost on that distant dome.

The colours fade, the pale blue sky grows higher.
Now I see the sun
Gradually rising
Over the rim of water-flat plain,
Bonfire bright, triumphant.
Soon I shall walk out
Through the white snow, dry as sugar
Into the real street.

Frederick Candelaria

Born 1929. Teaches at Simon Fraser University and edits *West Coast Review*. His first book of verse appeared in 1967 and his second is now ready for publication. A Canada Council Senior Fellowship recently enabled him to spend a year writing and studying in Spain.

Scuba Diving

In deep salt in the silent green slaughter-house,
an immense school of flat fish
hangs dumbly suspended, surprised in brine
like pickled tongues torn from lying mouths,
yours, mine, and everyone's but one—the one
we hear diving in dreams and silence when we
  surface.

Vogue

a straunge fasshion of forsaking

    in leather boots
dresses coats & gloves
    legions
of gamins urchins matrons
mannequins of fashion
fashion illusions
in plastic   skin   & hide
desired   loved   caressed

creased   wrinkled   cracked
bags   remaindered
in bargain basements

                    upstairs
strut   new models

Founded *Up th tube with one i (open)*—pomes, gotta book *Strange Movies (ive seen)*. Twenty-five in 1970. Now living in Vancouver where he paints and writes in a Cordova Street studio. Sings of going roothouse over the Bitch Goddess of Swat?

Chuck Carlson

Departure
CN & Great Northern Station

So so
yor leavng yu are
little blue travel bag awl packt
out in th white livng room
& yellow bag filld w/ sculpture
& litesho slides
me, sittng typng this
at yr CORONA portable on my 2nd beer
hearng yu splash across th hallway
in th big porcelain bathtub, bathng
yor softround body
all suds&cleanliness
i sit here batterng out this pome
& yu'll be gone 11 oclock
acrss th continent
yes . . . going & lookLOOK
Ime happy, reallyhappy *for* you!
I dont even take th time to ponder
if there'll be an emptiness, an aloneness
not even any apprehension anymore
Soon I'll to my Northern Christmas
,my mother, sister, brother & his newife
. . . a quiet refuge
Then
you come out of th bath damp, treat me royally
by presentng yor superb nakedness to me
to towel dry, drying yr damp head of hair
thru joyous breasts t belly

"gently . . .", you remind
,th dark kinkhair triangle thru to very toes
&
then
yu wrap th towel like an arab turban round yr head
and pose

beautiful womanly sculpture but
thet breaths, loves&touches me
oGod
tonight you are leavng. . . .

Lady Goat's Delirium

Medussa medussa o who'as seduced ya
& whose yr galley slave
Old wrought iron I walkt th lion
God, s'good t hear yu rave!

Jackson o jackson o where'as th action
th castle its crumbled t ruin
mad alice & ewart theyre comen t doit
tho Ceremony pauses til june

Where is my fife & wheres my drum &
where be my sidemen three
one three oclock jump, th birds in th dump
th other shot up w/ th Queen

Th rocking'as stopt, th bowling is not
a tall what th sandman means
if yu read in th book & watchen t look
yu'll see thet its all but a dream

Loony Tunes in My Ozone

I

One irly a-em th sidewalks buckled, trees came alive, houses danced & talkt with window mouths & light manifested itself—his urine was red then blue then green & th toilet outdid th walls fr my mystical brother. He's decided to stay home now, mindng th clocks, dustng rockers & such. . . .

My landlord makes wine & wundrs at th travel bureau i keep hidden in my desperate room. I try explaining about th gargoyles on th Vancouver Hotel whove been there a long time in th pissng rains. . . .

In vancouver autumns i pause on drake street and become only myself again after th psychosis of school hallways & profane poolhall beer festivals. . . .

With a bent mind i peer across false creek into th jumpng neons of th westend; a livr condition, longhaird & workng well i am, livng flip poetry moments and appreciating donalduck dostoevskisms. . . .

I want to return home fr awhile some day. In my mothers flat and carp over tea of LBJ and God and go out beltng along log haul highways in my rigskinner brothers Hayes smokemachine. . . .

Iull wander down streets of my boyhood undr blue city lights shaded by leafless trees, a white cold october moon in th starry skies, dreamng of our games, vacant lot conspiracys, our innocent madness & zests and feel sad. . . .

Returng home to wind th big hall clock, sip tea, pet th cat & when th fabricator & muck & uthr boyhood cohorts drop in weul sit & gt high in th little tv room watchng gt smart. . . .

I cn see meself when i grow old & dirty U/wear, talkng t meself, spittng in th gutter to escape hidng out in okanagan hills, remembrances of vivid youth scenes: turng into an old greybeard long-haird oldman wavng at CPR freights & cursing tobacco prices, eyeing yng girls of small-town mainstreet cafes. . . .

In th meantime wud yu miss me? write me? ask if i distill applecider & plum wine frm falltime orchards? Wud yu remember my maw & after-noon tea & my yng sis? ben webster on th record player?

2

Poets! theres enuf ugliness in th world. Dont thro beerbottles into hiway ditches or scratch hotel elevator doors nomatter who owns th bldg. Go out undr blue skies, plant flowers in desolation parks & paint yor door yellow, invitng birds to sing, i too miss my love!

Should yu barrel greyhoundbus in winternite snow iull refer yu to my uncle who advocates haircuts and *Time* to all yng artists. He's now a mortgage and an old mercedes, when i was a child he drew me terrific cartoons better then my own now. . . .

Its september in vancouver. Iull gt drunk with trotskyites again throwng up in their toilets to wake in th sunshine morning and wandr out into th little backyard marvelng at th patterns grape-vines make growng, broadway flashng by a block away. . . .

Will yu be waitng in th winter cold night, swingng clear starsplash sky, yor breath; steam risng in th crisp air, waitng t spy my hunchtup dufflecoatd form paddng along on dn th sidewalk to our secret smalltown meetng place, will yu be gleeful in yor heart and hug my woolytoggld middl & give me one kiss and say yor soglad?

Fred Cogswell

Born 1917. Professor of English at UNB. Former editor of *Fiddlehead*, current editor of *Humanities Association Bulletin*. Co-editor of *The Arts in New Brunswick* and *The Enchanted Land*. Editor of *Five New Brunswick Poems*. Editor and publisher of Fiddlehead Poetry Books. Books include: *The Stunted Strong*, *The Haloed Tree*, *The Testament of Cresseid*, *Descent from Eden*, *Lost Dimension*, *Star-People* and *Immortal Plowman*.

Obituaries

I look at obituaries

what interests me
are the figures
that tell me
the ages of the dead

If the ones I see
are less than mine
I am forced to stifle
a quick thrill of joy
at having outlived
a fellow human

If the number
I read is greater
I rejoice to think
of all the years
a man like me
may look forward to

but when the age
written there
is the same as my own
I shudder and wish
that there were no
obituaries

Last Letter

Dear General Nieh:

I am fatally ill.
I am going to die.
I have some last favours
to ask of you.

Tell them I have
been happy here,
and my only regret
is that I shall not
be able to do more.

My two cots are for
you and Mrs. Nieh.
My two pairs of English
shoes also go to you.

My riding boots and trousers
I should like to
give to General Lu.

Division Commander Ho
can select what he pleases
from among my things
as a memento from me.

I would like to give
a blanket each to
Shou, my attendant,
and Chang, my cook.

A pair of Japanese shoes
should also go to Shou.

We need 250 pounds of quinine
and 300 pounds of iron compounds

John Robert Colombo

Born 1936 in Kitchener, Ont. Managing editor, *Tamarack Review.* Member, Advisory Arts Panel, Canada Council. Author of *The Mackenzie Poems, Abracadabra, Miraculous Montages* and *The Great Wall of China* (translated into French by Jacques Godbout as *La Grande Muraille De Chine*). His most recent book, *John Toronto*, is a collection of found poems taken from the writings of John Strachan, the first Bishop of Toronto, of all people. An editor-at-large in Toronto.

each year. These are for
the malaria and anemia patients.

Never buy medicine
in such cities as
Paoting,
Tientsin and
Peiping again.
The prices there
are twice as much
as in Shanghai
and Hong Kong.

Tell them I have been
very happy. My only regret
is that I shall now
be unable to do more.

The last two years
have been the most significant,
the most meaningful years
of my life. Sometimes it
has been lonely, but I have
found my highest fulfilment
here among my beloved comrades.

I have no strength now
to write more. . . . To you
and to all my comrades,
a thousand thanks.

Norman Bethune

GO TO JAIL
MOVE DIRECTLY TO JAIL
DO NOT PASS "GO"
DO NOT COLLECT $200.00

GET OUT OF JAIL FREE
THIS CARD MAY BE KEPT
UNTIL NEEDED OR SOLD

MAKE GENERAL REPAIRS
ON ALL OF YOUR HOUSES
FOR EACH HOUSE PAY $25.00
FOR EACH HOTEL PAY $100.00

BANK ERROR IN YOUR FAVOUR
COLLECT $200.00

PAY SCHOOL TAX
OF $150.00

LIFE INSURANCE MATURES
COLLECT $100.00

PARKING FINE
$15.00

RECEIVE FOR SERVICES
$25.00

YOU ARE ASSESSED
FOR STREET REPAIRS
$40.00 PER HOUSE
$115.00 PER HOTEL

WE'RE OFF THE GOLD STANDARD
COLLECT $50.00

PAY A $10.00 FINE
OR TAKE A "CHANCE"

YOU HAVE WON SECOND PRIZE
IN A BEAUTY CONTEST
COLLECT $11.00

Professor of English at SFU. Author of *The Day of the Parrot* and *The Owl Behind the Door*, both published in 1968. His third and fourth volumes of poetry, *Cappelbaum's Dance* and *Cappelbaum's Lament* are in press for 1970. A full-length study of the literary twenties, *World War I and the American Novel*, was first published in 1967 and reissued in 1970. His fifth collection of poetry, *Elegy for the Love Generation*, is in preparation.

Stanley Cooperman

Cappelbaum Among the Cannibals

I

The grand piano in the belly:
mouths
with hairy tongues
hollering for
REAL talk,
girls or critics
with yellow birds
between their cheeks. . . .

Listen, I sniff every petal
with my own nose,
my words
are private as your underwear,
and the sound
of my breath grows
from my skull:

I plant my name
anywhere
I choose.

Reality? Sincerity? Truth?

Let me tell you, my
Reality
changes every time I
eat chicken,
I become something else
with every tit popped
at the sun, and
sometimes
there are grapes I peel
with the teeth
of my brain.

Don't tell me what SINCERITY
is, I carry it around
in my pants, under my collar:
whatever I say is made of paint
and kisses,
greasy dreams and REASONS
that grow like crabgrass on a pile
of cut
        poems.

2

Part of me is the splinter
under my toenails:
when I open my
voice, rabbits
eat pomegranates on a silk bed,
unicorns
raise their legs,
dying
under a shower of
apricots. . . .

What do you expect of a man
sailing
by the light of his own wind?

Let me tell you about
TRUTH:
it dances on the edge
of becoming, it
foams
on an ocean
of everybody's water turning
to air. . . .

Truth swims under the shadow
of stones,
like our faces

when we float toward each other
inside our separate balloons;

Truth is nothing, everything
that won't stand still for you,
for me, or the man
with cotton proclamations
wrapped
around his balls. . . .

WHY
should I swear who I am
when the whole thing
is not to decide

on this side of the grave?

Jenifer Waking

To drift is no
meaning: neither tree
nor root, and shapes of earth
held
in the circle
of your eye, are less
than light: an electric bulb
plugged
into stone.

Today
when you half-slept
in your skin,
putting on your robe,
drifting into the green light
of morning,

there was a rose
framed
in the small window
under your breast.

To drift
is no meaning: only
when I looked at you,
light
flowed green
between us: the glass
melted, the stone
dissolved
into white silk.

After the Protest Rally

And always the scream:
the corpse dancing with books
hanging
like iron bells
from the joints of his bones,
a smell
of rotted machines
turning to grass,
                    turning to grass
or proclamations
thin
as the flower
growing out of his eye.

When I walk through the street
there are old women
crucified
on telephone wires,
a sound of humming in the air

like mumbles of thick
laughter: and priests
with hooks
curved to the ends of their arms . . .
they hang
from their own blackness.

Even the snapdragons
bite one another,
fighting for room, fighting
for a deeper swallow
of light and air:
their colours
hammer the summer sun
with a fire of painted
teeth.

I was born in Toronto in 1932. Have had poems published, thanks to Fred Cogswell, Milton Wilson and James Reaney, in *Fiddlehead*, *Canadian Forum* and *Alphabet*. Have been working (longer than I care to admit) on a group of long poems built around the topography of Toronto.

Ralph Cunningham

Rockabye for Benny

mastoid gloves, eyes seagirth-moaned,
mashed-to-seabed brain dredged
by crowdexplosion wreckage,
clawed too far for mucus-blaze
of bell(as dead as puddle moon)to save,
can taste the alleyexits
jammed for good;
his cock

of fistcraft ham from jabs
the fierce in blow
that blew the bellies
up to ghettoes' poison odds,
crashing ringlight crowdpain
on its head;
toprope

womangraze his blades,
thighs puke into oceanknees
and no last wishes
swig his balls
of bread;
highsigns

to his biceps pissed
into skyless rivers, axed,
shoulder winched up higher than its sister,
pried again through furnace-rapids
eyes dissected surgeons claw no ask;

severed worm of leopard
in his skull
a spurting
purse.

O rows of sweat, you shellgame
as the stars believe
your guts

the witless panther too
will lick your light

as frail as ten.

Chinese

Basilisk and stolen eyings
traded from jade salmon sunset
to the weevil emperor
of night.

On their indented strayings
through our polity
gone silversquid
in river-flaked lanternscapes

on silk steeped in panes—
fish armour trickles
through the elders'
candled skulls

where the heronries
of mind like mist in glazes,
are the smoking wax of memory
in plumage all a spent and far tale's flight.

Down steps
ricepaper undertones
from cards
and lonely money

rustle men impaled
on the solicitude of chance;
and deep in tea-meek sallows,
from the petal-mastered

eons of the brain,
larvae'd colloquy violas
cello-curvature
of dark

while sapped by incense
(tea in boxes
frail as watercolour wings)
time refrains.

Stained-glassing
gutters' creased inkrain
(pressed ducks cra-
ckle glimmer darkly)

Gardens pinwheel
Dragons firestick
the flavours
of their offers

to the alien natives passing
who have never been moon-greenery
in cities' mute suspension
of the skin,

but not to sensibility
seeped into
the watercress of eyes
its years have fed,

from bramble-script cocoons
where silkworm and untombed
it eats the flower of its history
instead.

Born in Galt, Ont. in 1939. Published a book of poems in 1961, appeared in a number of small magazines about the same time, reviews for *Canadian Art*.

David Donnell

Giblets

For three days now I have wanted to write
a poem using the word giblets.
One thinks
automatically of chickens, lying on a cold table
they are plucked, of course, and their legs
are still trussed with a piece of twine.
The heads have not been severed,
are intact,
incongruous with the nude skin,
the red eyes
and the open throats
cut with a paring knife. The bird upside down,
a corner of the shed on my stepfather's farm,
the blood running down in thin streams

One thinks also of dogs. Their immediate colours
are black, brown, white, also perhaps liver.
This is the colour of dogness on my stepfather's
farm.
They mill around the table in a wave of colour,
assembling and dissembling,
basic shapes of aggression.

Pain is the psychological adjunct of a protective
reflex. It is at times not important to define

What I mean is abdominal paranoia,
how the stomach rebels against the head
while you whistle, cleaning
your knife on a small piece of burlap.

Tattoo

yesterday
I discovered you have been etched
on the roof of my mouth, venetian reds
and greens, some tuscan brown,
my mouth is a Sistine chapel now where
goats play in the aisles.
I am careful of what I eat and drink,
bread the colour of your brown skin
which reminds me of leaves,
oranges like your dress which leaves
the shoulders bare, wines
the colour of your red dress
which sets my black goat
with its bent horn, shrieking
like Michelangelo falling from his scaffold

A painted roof, a falling painter,
goats that cry out like roman poets,
when I laugh your hips arch like music
and my tongue moves in my mouth
to explore you.
My mouth
is where it's at, what spring comes to,
my mouth is the city of Florence
where the painter falls each time
he completes an image, where the goats
speak like roman poets,
where you always wear the orange dress
on Wednesdays

I write this
early in the morning, while the painter
is tying knots in the ropes of his scaffold,
thinking how nothing is less complex
than passion, how certain images become
larger during sleep, how, while you are
getting dressed in your own morning, sunlight

all over the rugs, the scaffold sways
with the same rhythm as your hips
and the sun is trapped in your bright hair
like an aztec bird;
enough light to paint by
while the goats eat their tin cans,
tumble about like spring undone
and knock down aisles, walls, brickwork,
scaffolds and this picture

Laying the Dust

I am hung by a green rope
in the middle of this May
running out of my veins like so much ale.
My Polish roominghouse settles
into the May dust,
its fat, brawn-friendly mistress
with her stockings rolled into sausages
and her bosom bursting its cotton
scrawled all over with flowers
like dutch bread
crumples the hall rug for roaches, dreaming
of mice the size of royal woodchucks,

I roll over in the comfortable dust
of spring, my heels ridged with horn,
dreaming of corn bread and fresh eggs,
Who could ask for a better home
in which to turn the heart around
with common things
and meander back, like Tom Fool,
to the burnt iron taste
of the heart imploding
its red minutes under the skin,
ridding itself of waste,

I put this rope around my neck
in March and wrote a brief note
to the Mayor:
                    I have greeted your proposal
of an East-West subway extension
with approval, but am still
disturbed about the absence of somewhere to go,
                    Your Fool, sir,
                    and the draft taps
                    are blithely swelling
                    as is my wife

Paul Dutton

Born 1943. Toronto Toronto Toronto. Three years at UWO. Cautious clerk. Quit. Supply teacher. Quit. Beginning to freelance. Like people, nature and peanut butter. Don't like suburbs, high-rise or big business (even peanut-butter big business). Like to sing (blues and traditional English folk) and give poetry readings. Plan poetry magazine with friends soon.

Neoma

Three and blonde
she will, being fond of beauty,
approach through the tall grass curtseying in the
  wind
with in her hands summer
as a gift of petals
cupped
and kept from spilling
in the very wind she invented with her feet
and honored to blow around her.

Free and blonde
she will, on the pond of summer air
float words that shall be
as the flight of a petal
swaying uncertainly down

and her laughter
singing in the wind
will be as the first sound heard
in the quietest world of dew.

The day will smile for not the last time
being wreathed in flowers
and she will curtsey like the grass
and present you
with a pool of summer
swaying in silence on lifting petals.

Jazz Musician

to James Moody

Adrenalin pusher
buying me dreams for a thought
selling me (thank you)
my own feelings I couldn't buy elsewhere
  and for payment only honesty that anyway
  you opened in me like a bloom
shoving them to me with (thank you)
enormous adornments
saying they're more beautiful than ever
than even I'd thought

and secondhand better
when writhed through a golden torture of—

You've taught me them
you
searched them out from
within you
and punch my brain with them

magnified

mutated

to purity

arpeggio river of saxsmooth velvet
hammering out metal to sumptuous smooth with
  only breath
rapids now over the drums' riff stutter
into eloquence
and float like a flower on thrumming bass pond

while (check) a grin (right) Amens your millenium
  (solid)

with (tell 'em, Preacher!) key chord
"Au'm hips."

And *I'm* hip:

my head can't divide it
but the rest of me can tell
knows you'll have nudged when I'm sleeping
from their diamondhard settings
the most shattering dreams I've kept hidden:

tell it to me now
tell it to me now
tell it to me now
now
now
now
broken rhythms, cacophonic order
each
smashed riff
angerstroked
bleeds beauty

proves fallen
with each building blow
what
who? me? yes. what? us? yes.
had (why?) thought sure

most daring
you balance on the razor-edge
of time
with a horn
and hellfire
resplendent
uncompromising prophet

time your measure
time your master
knitting you together time

being knit
time folded
unfolding you
  time's master
  time's measure

knocking out barnacled emotions
from some ship's graveyard
for the stifled primal
oh! to set them swaying in an ocean of notes

(I'm carried up leagues of sound
forced to use music for breathing)

they're body juice now
running thick
intuitive groove

into it I've grooved
knocked out
taught
what was all unlearned
now know like a river

Oh! didn it rain! (Oh! didn it rain!)
Oh! didn it rain! (Oh! didn it   didn it   didn it

Maurits Escher

1 × 2 is 2 × 1 × 1 is 1 × 1 × 2 is 2 × 1
and
you drew
the devil staring your skull in the eye
and
"knowing nothing of the real world"
you

stare death straight in the mirror
and don't need Russia
or the U.S.A.
but
know he's only in
the iris of your eye;
eat the apple
spit out the seeds
stare death down
and walk unworried
in your fantastic world
you
perpetually possible in an impossible world
are
2 × 1 is 1 × 1 × 2 is 2 × 1 × 1 is 1 × 2

Maurits Escher, a Dutch graphic artist who creates symmetrical designs of interlocking figures which evolve from side to side into backgrounds for each other, has drawn a self-portrait with a death's-head in the iris. He points out that, since man is always confronted with Death, Death must be standing in front of him and so would be reflected in the blackness of the eye.

The Man Who Married Colvin Kell

Deborah Eibel was born in Montreal in 1940 and educated at McGill and Radcliffe. In 1965 she was awarded the Arthur Davison Ficke Sonnet Prize of the Poetry Society of America. In 1967 and 1968 she worked on a book of poems under a Canada Council Arts Bursary. Her work has appeared in *Audit*, *Approach*, *Dalhousie Review*, *Red Clay Reader*, *Malahat Review*, *New Voices of the Commonwealth*.

Deborah Eibel

After a spinsterhood of many years,
Colvin Kell, the illiterate charwoman
Who spoke in the dictum
Of those initiated by the wind,
Who never worried about decorum,
Accepted the offer of an unlikely man,
One who had been rejected by other charwomen,
Because he was shiftless.
But Colvin Kell, being a grammarian among
  charwomen,
Could read his mind.
Because she used the wind as "vade-mecum," as
  gloss,
He was never too inscrutable for her.
She accepted him, because he was a whole man:
He loved caterpillar and moth and butterfly,
Wood and fire and ash.

Late marriage was meaningful
In ways that earlier marriage could not have been.
The pastimes that mattered now
Could not have mattered before.
Nothing could have mattered before.
They loved to walk in stony places:
They verified themselves by kicking stones.
They honoured each other.
She kept the floors and walls and woodwork
Immaculate for him.
Delighted with her art,
He scratched "Colvin fecit"
On whatever she touched.
(These are the only words she ever learned to
  read.)
He paid further tribute
By playing his flute.
When she asked him
Why he repeated the melody hour after hour

Without embellishing it,
He said that for this theme
There could be no variations.

But one day, years later,
When he thought her back was turned,
He changed.
She understood what was happening.
She had known from the first
That a change must come about, sooner or later,
That he would one day lean away, break away.
(After all, had he not married beneath his station?)
That day, he did not ask her to go walking with
 him,
But she left the kitchen anyway and followed at a
 distance.
There were stones on the road;
He walked around them instead of kicking them.
He embellished the flute melody,
For which, he had said before,
There could be no variations.

It was dark, it was raining, he was old.
He agreed to come home.
He went to sleep.
Colvin Kell knew that he was searching
For a carnival place, for hilarity.
They would not meet again, anywhere.
(She did not mean that he was necessarily lost,
For he had not been a worthless man.
But there would always be distance between
 them.)

Just before he left,
All seasons converged on his tongue.
After his departure, they realigned themselves.

Born Oshawa 1903, lives in Montreal. *Three Dozen Poems* (1957), *A Lattice for Momos* (1958), *Blind Man's Holiday* (1963), *Four Poems* (1963), *Wrestle with an Angel* (1965), *Incident on Côte Des Neiges* (1966), *Raby Head* (1967), *The Dark Is Not So Dark* (1969).

R. G. Everson

The Chance-taking Dead

A field of Ontario Quaker graves
very old
no headstones
nothing showing where the graves are

An acre or more of grassland
intense with devout dead
who entered underground
on their own plan to lie unknown

In this uneven field
some mounds of longer grass
two dying elms
a few protruding glacial stones

No new graves
Congregation gone
Religion gone
They entered underground to lie unknown
on their own plan
I stare at the chance-taking dead

On & On Beyond Whitemud & Stone Pile Post

On & on out of Alberta
into Saskatchewan
running
without pulling up   running wildly

Under our whirlybird over the grey Cypress Hills
an antelope jumping
from shadows of alders & on ahead of our whirling

antelope running in dust
leaping over willows
on & on out of any home area

This whitepatch pronghorn is running south of
Fort Walsh
& slanting away in newly-forming shapes
for the Old-Man-On-His-Back Hills

Our earth revolves in 4 minutes less than 24 hours
in a year goes around the sun 600 million miles
Time is an antelope
running on & on out of my mind

Our earth axis turns around
in 26,000 years
the two poles wandering on circles 40 miles wide

We go on & on at 12 miles a second with our sun
at 170 miles a second with our galaxy
on & on among newly-forming galaxies
that jump up from the dust of the universe

We whirl out of our minds in dust beyond the
Cypress Hills
over Whitemud
over Stone Pile Post

over War Holes
over Pinto Horse Butte
over Wood Mountain
over Willow Bunch Lake

We whirl with the dust of our minds
newly-forming
among quasars at the speed of light

How Wonderful to Hear that Human Sound

On a snake-slighter meadow
cold in moonlight
alongside squidshark ocean
where barnacles in empty tidepools
close their towers
these overnight cabins are away from one another

I hear commotions of a water closet
from a far cabin

Our washrooms are connected underground
How wonderful to hear the human sound

I was carried here in machinery
on divided highways
to avoid running into anyone

Last week a woman spoke to me
saying Route 17
saying 420 miles
saying 19 miles to a gallon

She said It's dreadful going near to Boston
She said Keep away from LA
Toronto Ottawa Oshawa

Out this cabin window
stars of the Milky Way appear together
If we get there
likely all worlds will be far from one another

but I have heard constellations colliding in Vega

She said Don't go
near Chicago
Keep away from Vancouver

The washrooms are connected underground
How wonderful to hear that human sound

Born in Budapest in 1910. Listed under *Hungarian Literature* in the *Encyclopedia Britannica* as one of the "five most talented poets of the post-war era." His works in English include an autobiography, *My Happy Days in Hell* (1963) and a forthcoming biography of Erasmus. His sonnets were first published in the original by Irodalmi Ujsag in Paris.

George Faludi

The Third Sonnet

I swing, strung from your shoulders:
in your deep eyes I suicide.
I drop my defences and on my knees
I surrender with a kleenex.

I strip off more than clothes.
I expose myself: bare-naked,
mother-naked. My only defence
is my delicious lack of defence.

I again renounce my friends, even my son,
the way I did when first we met.
That meeting! Let me lick your ankle.

Let me grovel. Like a teenager,
let me grope at your toes and grow up:
ah, my forehead is circled with stars!

Translated from the Hungarian by John Robert Colombo

The Seventy-first Sonnet

From the corners of your eyes youth sends
plum-blue flickers of pain toward me.
If I had any honour at all
I'd stay away from your sweet mouth.

Perhaps even now it's not too late
for me to shake off your hang-dog loyalty and
throw you out.
Poor lunatic, what do you expect
from me, a poet, in a room between cracked walls?

Is it my face you love, puckered with poverty?
Wake up and look ahead.
All I can leave you here is horror
when the worn puppet tumbles down.

Take your hand from my yellow hand
where the water of time is trickling out.

Translated from the Hungarian by R. G. Everson

The Twelfth Sonnet

Like a cobalt shadow at your ankles, space grew.
And in the universe: nothing. Nothing but you.
The clock stops. Beyond your shoulder
The palm trees explode, and are not true.

At the window, performance of the light-ballet,
Your face engages passage of today,
Jasmine from your shoulder names the month.
Our neighbours are beyond the Milky Way.

Furniture, like weightless trapezes and empty
  tents,
Float and flap between us. When I turn:
Dust is falling on five continents.

Then nothing but the torque of your presence in
  the room,
Below: loquacious calm of the sea,
Above: pirouettes and pirouettes of the moon.

Translated from the Hungarian by J. Michael Yates

The Thirty-sixth Sonnet

Starved lion of my passion, savage beast of prey
padding this jungle on its four soft feet
hot for your love. Now my lips on their way
to yours graze your throat. Days and nights never
meet

while I explore you. Your body looms between,
barrier to love. O it's plain you're not there
when we touch. But you sleep in vain. Behind
your screen
of secret burning flesh I track you down unaware.

Raw bitch, for you I'll neither pray nor wish evil,
my pact with your soul makes me out the Devil;
why care for your cheap nakedness, the lean

melons of your buttocks, freckled shoulders?
Rather say
that I turn from you to find you, somehow mean
in closing my eyes to see you better elsewhere.

Adapted from the Hungarian by Raymond Souster

Fetherling was born in the States in 1947 and has hitch-hiked across a great part of North America. Has worked as a newspaper reporter, editor and radio scriptwriter. Now living in Toronto, he's the author of *the united states of heaven/gwendolyn papers/that chain-letter hiway* and *Fugitive Poems.*

Doug Fetherling

Spécialité de la maison poème

all the great men have eaten shrivelled
hamburgers here at the varsity restaurant
one of two convenient locations to
serve u better if they
serve u at all
i recall all the great men of the arts
in twos or threes
interrupting themselves to order the
number one special from
snarky waitresses w/
varnished eyes

& the young poets too
gulping acid cokes   paying quickly   &
dashing out to bloor&spadina only to
be arrested moments later for
driving under the influence of
leonard cohen

Both Down and Out in Old Toronto, Tho Principally Down

discrepancies in another's ideology of literature
    found
me hitting all the pawnshops on church street
trying to get a few dollars for a rusty wristwatch
    laurel
found on a beach in jamaica in 1962

i referred one seedy gentleman of hebrew
extraction to the original greek after he

questioned my pronunciation of "omega" &
left w/ three dollars in pieces of silver to
pacify my fingertips as i
walked w/ the wind across dundas square

it looks now as if tomorrow is going
to be a rough winter:
by monday ill be returning my
beer bottles for the deposit which
at 2¢ apiece should keep me going
until i find contribution to the united
church observer joke page a fi-
nancial necessity
but it always has been my policy not to let
starvation
interfere with the execution of vers libre

John Glassco was born in Montreal in 1909. Books: *The Deficit Made Flesh* (1958), *A Point of Sky* (1964). Forthcoming: *The Poetry of French Canada in Translation* (1970), an anthology.

John Glassco

Ceremony

1

Lower your voice: we are passing the school for
  the deaf.
Raise your hand to a horrible acquaintance.
Lower your eyes: we are passing the workshop of
  the blind.
Raise your lips to that old whore's painted face.
Lower your head: we are passing the city
  madhouse.
Raise your hat to the shining hearse.

So shall we enter into the mansions of the just
And dwell for a moment within the holy mountain
Of the pitiful, the ceremonious,
Who acknowledge, without accepting, all the
  imperfections
Whether of mind or body, only by these gestures
Which are all we have, and whose performance
Is the one ritual binding us together, the quick,
  the damned and the dead.

The ceremony of the dry martini
Is also important. Chill the glasses.
Observe the right proportion of ingredients. Stir
  slowly.
Strain, pour. And then
Drink to each other with the lips
Which are also the lips of love
To be loosened in delightful discourse
Which is also the measure of a certain music,
Of the intellectual spaces and the spheres
Dividing and joining in such perfect interrelations
As make Chaos and Old Night gnash their dry
  disorderly teeth.

2

Despair, too, is struck down by ceremony,
Nor can pale dejection stand against it.
Madness itself is beaten down by ceremony,
The jewel not found in the earth but fashioned
Out of earth and shining from the hands that
made it,
The hands of all men who equate measure with
solace,
And the formal, always, with the good;
Who striving forever in the flux and darkness
To establish a congruency between their atoms
and their actions,
Between the eternity of their dreams
And the doomed pulses they inherit,
Simply raise and lower the flag of their hearts.

Not too long is the road before us
This street that must be made a meadow
This money that must be turned to beauty
These maladies and tortures that must be driven
back to their paternal darkness,
But not too short for a man to raise his hand
Against the evil Accuser of this world
The everlasting tempter and adversary
Whose peace is in negation and indifference
Whose work is done by the cool abstracted stare.

The Women of Quebec

Born in 1917 of Canadian parents in London, England. Six books of poems have appeared since 1954. The two most recent: *A Friction of Lights* (1963), *Pictures on the Skin* (1967). Now living in Vancouver and working on his *Selected Poems.*

Eldon Grier

Once they lay breeding as the sky pried open the
shell of winter.

Once they lay breeding the arms of the evergreens
pinioned with snow.

Once they lay breeding the threat of death like a
coffee stain.

Once they lay breeding nostalgia stamping in the
threshold.

Once they lay breeding the bellwinch summoning
the forest.

Once they lay breeding the martyr's wit.

Once they lay breeding the sour dawns the flour
of misery rising in the cradles.

Once they lay breeding the tribal scar their bodies
of rush in America's vein.

Once they lay breeding the pungent smell of
slavery in their hair.

Once they lay breeding the crackle of billboard
pistols and gum.

Once they lay breeding the terrible chansons of
their fate.

Once they lay breeding collections of grist and
plastic revolution.

Once they lay breeding a film in which everyone
was a negress.

Once they lay breeding the eye of the ptarmigan
the plumasier's tunic.

Salute for Gerry Rodolitz

A spiel of grace, an early sunprick for the imagined
river;
so it begins as it begins for all the others;
long-drawn sound of traffic,
milk bomb at the door, woman coughing uphaa
uphaa uphaa.

Barring the way the moss-red brick of Care,
grocery window through
which you silently crash swimming into the blood,
morning hallucination
at which I have stared dumbfounded by its
opacity.

Once you started to read the "sickness" disappeared
Light from the floor
became attentive. The bed stopped ingesting you
through its labial tissues.
In fish-bright plane the courier sang. Rimbaud,
Artaud, assembled at poem's weightless plunge.
The poem slowly withdrawn as if the Under-
ground, your Love, had threatened a burning.

Perhaps I exaggerate, perhaps I was thrown at
finding so unexpectedly, so perfectly
a brother so terribly open like a wound. The
courier, your pimp-dead girl,
lost in physical blue her half-breasts plastered
noons, her mouth of lights unyielding
like a thousand bloodied trilliums.

Gerry Rodolitz with sickness-spaniel hair, six
containers of pills by unmade bed,
I want your recipe for incense, your
Ginsberg-goddess landed,
I want your twenty-seven years in which you are
dying live and unchanging.

Born 1909 in the Eastern Townships of Quebec. Studied at Bishop's University, where he now teaches, and at Oxford. Author of five books of poetry, the latest, *Ixion's Wheel* (1969). Editor of *The Penguin Book of Canadian Verse*. Music critic for the CBC.

Ralph Gustafson

Nocturne: Prague 1968

1

The fields are cool
and the shadows on the fields
yield to the wind and sun.
Then, it was early August,
Prague, a hundred miles
over these green fields,
over Franconia,
and the grass free to the winds
and the winds to the sky. . . .

2

The promises at Cierna,
the promises at Bratislava,
who would keep them,
the walls frightened,
the rooms of little men,
the rooms of Moscow,
Brezhnev stuttering
with anger,
white with anger,
holding up the flowers
at the station at Bratislava,
yielding on all important points,
the white dagger of Czechoslovakia,
the green fields of Czechoslovakia,
pointing to the heart of Russia,
the closed rooms,
shadows in the Kremlin;
the green fields,
the shadows of the sun
in the frightened rooms;
who would keep those promises,

the stones frightened,
the walls frightened,
the walls of Berlin?

3

There were sounds in the night,
the shadows of night,
the treads on the road,
the wheel-treads in the streets.
In Ruzyne Street
a cat tipped over the pail of garbage.
A tank knocked down a lamppost.

4

Spring has come to an end,
as it will do,
in late August.
There is no denying that summer ends
when the grain is taken in,
and the fields are rough,
and there is no longer sun
and shadows in the waving grain.

5

There is always love,
small talk at the bars,
arguments, amiable enough
though serious,
at the factory, in the schools,
conventions, not entirely serious,
and casting one's vote—
to get rid of the talk.
There is reason,
and reasonable acceptance.

Spring need not end in January.
Much can be done.

6

Then there is force,
there is steel
and orders
given to young men
not knowing much about it
but obeying orders,
going to a new country,
to new streets,
comforted by steel
and looking forward to girls
and talk and beer at the tables,
well-meaning enough,
doing what they are told
but enjoying it.

7

There is always the possibility
of crushing an idea.

8

The young woman from Mrakov
with her toy rifle
guarding the local frontier
can be dealt with.
It was always the custom for Mrakov
symbolically to guard the region,
but she can be dealt with,
and the minds of a people,
with their ideas,
the young and the old,

the lovers,
the fringe
listening to The Fluff,
the rock group booked
into the Vysokoskolsk Klub
for a three-week stand.

9

The streets were taken in a night.
Despite the fact that it was unexpected
it was incredibly efficient.
The mild and ideologically quiet Dubcek
was in manacles by morning.

10

What is needed for an idea
is a little planning,
a few flowers.

11

It was a period of euphoria.
A miniskirted girl pushed a baby stroller,
someone sat on a statue,
a student read,
some poet wrote a poem
about fields, green fields,
Ruzena Polakova, a red-haired model
in hostess pyjamas,
draped herself against an ancient
garden wall,
journalists turned out the news,
professors asked about things.
It was all a cliché.

12

Brezhnev, Kosygin and Podgorny
consulted the generals.

13

In the West
there was consternation
but the situation was delicate,
there could be excuses for oppression,
someone might get angry,
all that was needed for more tanks
was an expression of sympathy.
There might be a setback.
Johnson listened to Dobrynin
impassively.

14

Smrkovsky, chairman of the National Assembly,
told the nation
although "we knew we would have
to pay a price for it,
we did not know the price would be
so terrible."

15

In some way it would be possible
to continue the "spirit of January,"
though at a reduced speed,
the leaders told the people.

16

What is it possible to propose
against tanks, against armour
on the roads, in the streets of Czechoslovakia?
Green fields? September?
A proclamation of seasons?
Steadier, more reliable
than ritual of flowers
is metal,
revolving turrets,
pragmatic sun.
What shall we stop them with?
Carnations at Bratislava?
There is no known weapon to counter tanks.
This is a restrictive fact
known to those who own tanks.

17

In downtown Prague
they put garbage on the hot engines.

18

Bratislava
free radio
station: "Our contempt is stronger."

Svoboda: "There is no way back
from freedom and democracy."

Jan Hus: "Love the Truth. Let others
have their truth,
and the truth will prevail."

Hitler: "The more they curb themselves,
the more dangerous they become."

19

Spit, Czechs!
Slovaks!
Clear your throat, grandmother!
Fill your streets!
Switch around the street signs!
Take house numbers from the doors!
Smother them in fraternal attentions!
Welcome the treads!
Return that love!
Professor, tear up paper!
You, mother, say that you do not understand
Russian!
You, students, spike the turret guns with
broomsticks!
As you did.

20

The square of Vaclav is washed,
the statue is washed of paint:
Russians, go home.
Nothing is heard in the great square.
No sound of provocation.
The streets of a people,
of a million people,
are a map.
No sound of consolation.
No word of grievance.

21

In late autumn,
on the shores of the Massawippi,
it comes home
to my mind,
the denial, even the intimacy of
love, now,
when Prague
is silent.

Born in Point Edward, Ont. in 1937. In 1960 graduated from UWO in honours English. Taught high school for seven years. Now Assistant Professor of English at Althouse College of Education. Books: *Riel: a Poem for Voices* (1968), *The Village Within* (1969).

Don Gutteridge

Riel

There is no
eloquence to
blood running
from the mouths
of wounds and
battles lost,
the eyes
of the dead
at Duck Lake
and Batoche are
white stones
darkening
at
the
centre.

I hear
no story
of their suffering
no rhythm
of waters running
blue St. Lawrence
breathing tides
the earth-red
of my own river
blending
to seed of lakes
the world
may wait
a hundred suns
to see

When my body
swings like a
dead tongue
from the white-man's

scaffolding,
will there be
an eloquence
to tell . . .

or will this
prairie be
a coffin
for my voice
a dwelling place
for
  two
    white
      stones?

Born in Toronto in 1938. Brought up there and in Niagara-on-the-Lake. University of Toronto. Liverpool 1960–62. Kingston since 1962. Spent last year in England. Books: *Figures in a Landscape* (1968), *The Streets of Summer* and *The Sign of the Gunman* (both 1969).

David Helwig

Poem in Acoustic Space

I am listening to time
moving through me, against me,
and to the singing
of your body in my hands.

Time is music on the skin
and the movement of my hands
finding the soft and smooth
and rough textures of you

is light in the mind.
You are continuous
as the universe
as I discover you

and I become the endless
light of where you are
and you are everywhere
through the time of time.

Elegy

. . . later I found out that Julio Zenon Acosta had died on the hilltop. That uneducated and illiterate quajiro *who had understood the enormous tasks which the Revolution would face after its victory, and who was learning the alphabet to prepare himself for this, would never finish that task*

—Che Guevara

Julio Zenon Acosta, did the Cuban bugs
pick your bones on that jungle hilltop

where you died twelve years ago?
Did the green snakes coil in your ribs?

In the days before that day
you walked through the dangerous hills
carrying supplies and the weight
of your gigantic hopes, one by one
adding the letters of the alphabet
to your kit. Dying too soon
your death was a silence, a screaming
hole in the world on a Cuban hilltop.

Waiting on that hilltop
at forty-five years old,
a peasant who gave his love
to the words of strangers
was killed in a surprise attack.

A man had betrayed your comrades. They ran
into the green of the deeper forest,
left blankets, medical supplies
and left your body,
one letter in a nightmare language
written on a Cuban hill
where your hope of words ended.

Twelve years later, Julio Acosta,
I imagine your bleached bones
somewhere in Cuba and your body
part of the Cuban earth, and I bring
these letters of my foreign alphabet
to speak of your interrupted task
and your wordless death.

A Fragment from Sappho

Being a god, that's what it's like
to sit with you and listen from close by
to the way you talk, to hear you laugh.
My heart pounds in my ribs.

And when I look at you I stammer, can't speak,
my tongue is paralysed, or I look
and a cold fire runs over my skin,
I sweat, can't see right or hear,
or I start to shake, turn pale,
sick, green as grass.
Sometimes I think I'm dying.

(And now I must learn to be content
with poverty, with separation.)

Born 1946. From Halifax and Wolfville, NS His poetry appears in *Quarry*, *Alphabet*, *Fiddlehead*, *Canadian Forum* and *Prism*. He's currently in Toronto completing a novel.

Bill Howell

Troubadour

for Ernest Buckler

Your part of listening is feeling, being
happy for him here, hearing him smile to
leave his time alone.
This strange man who speaks today of
many knows the best of many, too,
once he starts his singing.
He mixes music with friends instead of words,
so his songs are sad while you wait for
the best of tunes to come.

He always finds he has to leave himself
inside his songs, has to find himself
outside their timeless changes.
His new songs are sweet with the land of
yesterday, and his old ones still hold you
quiet now as he comes by.
Yes, he's loved enough to sing about it
afterwards, and in his time he's learned that
words are not enough for going on.

Do you feel his passing?

The Long and the Short

It's the start of a new snowball.
It's crunching around in leaves in the old
fashioned places kids always seem to find
and grow up from. It's when everything's dead
as soon as it hits the backstop. It's how long

it's been since wondering what it's like up there
at the other end of the kitestring, the end
that never stops. It's a year ago.

The Handle of Tomorrow

Will I lie
quietly with an arrow
in my heart,
my body growing cold
without my words, however true,
to warm me?

CENTRELEA, ANNAPOLIS COUNTY:
And still today I come after Blood Creek
with the record of the water running
thick and scarlet in the sun—
a day away from Acadia.
The report of the day is in my hand
and its arrows, pounding in the air,
sort themselves out—this for another,
this one for me.

This was the French side
   with the Micmacs with their dogs.
That was this English side
   with the water running quicker with the
      ambushed drums
toward the greater sea of meetings
as it does as I stand alone
   with other arrows flying here.

I become my own history watching itself:
the well-appointed Red of my forefathers marching
in strict time toward my time, now

back with the blood Red Micmacs moving
stealthily—at least, I know now, the Micmacs
of the mind.

All of us surely die in our own way,
a matter of our own matter, this time:
June 10, 1711.
My arrow.
Quicker, stronger, straighter the always shaft,
always unseen comings
and goings.

Then the question of the captive and the wounded . . .

WHAT ALWAYS HAPPENS?

. . . the torture of the mind in killing and dying in ideas
of ourselves and freedoms from forevers and infinities
of pain—joy acclaiming itself, if we live.

CAPE BLOMIDON, KING'S COUNTY:
And still today I come before Glooscap
where I look down at where I study
the Micmac god and warrior chieftain. HE
is fiercer than fierce, blood redder than any
brothers, mightier and truer, higher
and low, and dead.

Can I, perhaps, escape
itealthily,
snto the fur forests of fortune?
Or run beside their memory
like an Indian dog
with a bloody Red Coat soldier's right
arm clamped firmly
in my jaws?

Mechanics of Living

Becoming each other with flatteries and swearing
words with yellow endings, you lie
toward me with decency
enough to make love, while I
leave my glasses on to see you better
from my distance, running the risk
of breaking them
while we bury ourselves
in this process.

Born in Ottawa in 1934. Studied at Carleton. Now Master in English and Assistant Chairman, General Arts and Science, Centennial College. Books: *Burglar Tools* (1963), "The Seasons of Miss Nicky" in *Two Longer Poems* (1965), *Total War* (1967), *Fragments of the Dance* (1969).

Harry Howith

Priorities

in memoriam Daniel Knight

A classic carcinoma is deployed
through my friend's lymph and marrow;
he, devout Catholic, doubtless
prays privately to reconcile
God's sparrow-charity with slow
twenty-six-year-old dying, but

with visitors at his hospital bed,
between chemotherapy and radiation,
he jokes about the cigarette machine
in the lobby, and bears with love
memorial dreams of health that flicker
sometimes in his lovely wife's clear eyes.

Meanwhile, twisting wire coathangers
into fantastical and meaningless mandalas,
I bitch about going broke
on ten thousand a year, and listen to you
fret on your psychological guitar
about "more honest human relationships."

Hobbling on canes my cancer-blasted friend
lights candles for our conversion,
as I light up another cigarette,
and you light up another epigram,
and many ingenious sick cells
strangle his body and our souls.

If this is seemly,
loan me twenty bucks till payday.

On My Thirty-fourth Birthday

Your kiss congratulates my shuffling
that much closer to my death,

which, I intuit, will be ordinary
as eating an apple. Significant

only for the extraordinary
(Lumumba, Malcolm X, Guevara)

who didn't spend birthdays
writing poems, my own obit

is rehearsed every year under Leo,
in any season that sprouts writing

or loving. But it's no hassle:
I cannot imagine even a raccoon

living forever; the very intimation
of immortality is repugnant.

Therefore do not protest, but
understand that we mourn only our own

prospects, at least until we learn
the propriety of all codas.

Here, little darling, is my warm hand:
give me your shivering fingers.

The Grass is Browner

This evening, against music terribly clear,
I am brought news that you, also, smoke:
but only, it is reported, with friends.

One way or another I am always high.
After ten years, I prefer visions which permit
perfect reconstruction of your detailed body,

in this memory too facilely smothered
by interlocutory affections, and by
final decrees on the mutability of candles.

Understand that I do not invariably giggle.
Usually I must be stoned to stillness
before the evidence of your architectonic body

is admissible here, in a wing chair, bare
toes pointing toward the record player, where
is cut the saline satire of the Mothers,

offering solutions for children borne
after opportunity was somehow mislaid. . . .
The Prime Minister does not smoke, also

detests tobacco, drinks rarely, but has
the comforts of the mattress and of power.
Do not begrudge me, powerless, my surrogates.

Still needing you, I smoke or ball with anyone.

Born London, England, 1930. Came to Canada 1956, lives in Vancouver, lectures at UBC. *Three Ring Circus Songs*, first volume of poetry, published 1968. Other work (poetry, prose, criticism) in many Canadian magazines.

John Hulcoop

two poems from andrew wyeth's world: an exploration

1

wide, wide as the wings of the water-colour sky
two pages wide, andrew wyeth
brush strokes as long as the eye can see
and barely trees; a rabble of birds
breaking away from the up-hill horizon:
the path you take through a field
in the winter bare world of william penn
swinging down from (is it adam johnson's
over the far white hump of a hill
that disappears like moby dick in moonlight
as you descend from) the ridge
where rooks are rising and calling
to the wide expanse of unpainted paper
(is it archie's corner or the bottomlands)
is white, andrew wyeth, as white
as the disappearing hill is white
as the sky above the distant ridge is white
white, two pages white

2

down the hill

"all topsy-turvy like a rolling stone"
you say and I see
an ugly boy in an ugly boy's hat
wearing what could be an old army jacket
with big brass buttons, blue cords and boots
that leave less of a mark
on the hard winter ground
than the delicate shadow, frantic and thin
flying behind him

is it you, andrew wyeth
or is it allan lynch, lurching
down the hill across the wheel tracks
in towards the wood and wire fence

who is it really
running down
at a loss
and away from what

what did he see
when he stood in the winter of forty six
on the other side of the ominous hill
that grows more like stone
every time you paint it

a portrait of him:
man's head with meat hook
called karl

a dead deer strung by the neck
and hanging from a fragile tree
like a lynched corpse, the ground gory
a bucketful of guts freezing under the falling snow

or the imagined sight
of a free hand floating
in a final fastidious gesture
a painter's hand groping
to find something hard, something familiar to
hold on to
while the last of his great life laboured
in the huge man's frame to give birth
to death on a railway crossing

an ugly boy's beautiful hand
not even cold though it was winter
and innocent still though years later
allan lynch turned his delicate hand against himself
stopped his shadow in its tracks

Born in Hungary in 1935. Came to Canada in 1956. Works for CBC Toronto, and besides poetry has written several radio and television plays. Has published poetry in many Canadian magazines and in such anthologies as *New Wave Canada*, *The Penguin Book of Canadian Verse*, *The Oxford Book of Modern Canadian Verse*, *The New Romans*, *The Blasted Pine*, *Notes for a Native Land*. His first collection of poems, *The Absolute Smile*, was published in 1967, his second, *The Happy Hungry Man*, in 1970.

George Jonas

Three Sections from *The Happy Hungry Man*

1. AMERICAN GIRL: A CANADIAN VIEW

It is reassuring
To spend part of a night
With an American girl.

Chances are she will not resemble
The leaders of her nation
In speech, figure or stance:

If she has imperialistic designs
She may draw you without a struggle
Into her sphere of influence.

Then you'll find her battledress
Fit for her private battles,
See not her battleships but hear her battlecries,
And melt (perhaps with a wistful smile)
Before the native napalm of her eyes.

But she'll seem to be prepared
To give as well as to accept
Some foreign aid

And by midnight or so
While the fires of her manifest destiny smoulder
You'll be all ready to slip across
The world's longest undefended border.

2. FOUR STANZAS ON SALVATION

If God is dead
Perhaps we'll all go to heaven.
Michael the queer, Iris the scrotum-stroker
Will mix with older angels in the wide
Windless expanse of paradise.

It will be nice to bask in static bliss
After the twisting pleasures of our lives.
Having flown rockets over sleeping towns
We have more need of Eden than the saints.

Children we burnt will wait for us with flowers
And look politely at the crystal foam
Around our mouths, and lead us by the hand
To see the spot where God's throne used to stand.

We will forgive ourselves for we are good.
If this is heaven, we'll make the best of it.
There must be music of a kind, there must be sex,
And refreshments will be served at ten to six.

3. THE CNR VIRGIN

Women don't travel in clubcars
Young and innocent women especially don't
Salesmen travel in clubcars
And junior executives who don't rate airplane
  tickets
And senior executives who do but have heart
  conditions
So the girl in this clubcar is sitting pretty
The conductor gives her his full attention
Causes a little table to be lowered beside her
And personally tenders her a glass of tomato juice
And stands by until the rim of the glass
Has safely found its way to her suspicious lips.
Meanwhile the train moves onward to Montreal
Ancient forests yield to its passing
One can hear the wheels whispering to the axles
Did you know we have a virgin in the clubcar?
Soon she will respond to the last call for lunch
A happy piece of salmon will sit in her plate
Which she may reward with half a gentle smile.

Born 1929, teaches at the Université de Sherbrooke, lives in North Hatley, Que. Books: *Frost on the Sun* (1957), *The Sun is Axe-man* (1961) and *Phrases from Orpheus* (1967). Has recently completed a book on Canadian literature.

D. G. Jones

To Tory

21/3/69

I sit in a room with chairs
and tables, last
year's autumn leaves
and dried wildflowers,
late.

The world
continues on its wobbly course
and water drips
in the fireplace—spring
announcing itself.

The fire is out.

When you sat
silent on the end of the couch
your hair spilled,
deliberately, over your face
it flamed.

Now you're in bed.

A good thing. Still,
I've nothing to say, no
advice
on how to be happy, what
to expect in a world
violent enough,
mixed.

Except, there is no
terror here. Spring
drips in the chimney, gurgles
outside somewhere
beyond the wall.

Not that you wanted advice.

Tonight
the ash in the grate is not
final, no fire
is needed, the dried flowers
are still
delicate. Sleep.

The earth turns
gently on its wobbly course.

The Route Out

It is the route out, where
oil sludge mixes with the sea,

a loneliness.

The creek accepts
our beer cans, cardboard, parts of trucks.

It is a breakdown and escape,
this wilderness.

It is the field of wrecks,

the sunlight on the broken glass, a girl
half-dressed
who fumbles at a young man's pants, Christ, socks
his clothing stuck
on vinyl. Free
his cock contains her. Night
may whistle in the weeds.

It is the clutch.

And the advance, through small fires.

It is the route across the garbage dump
amid the flames, and smoke, and low cloud.

These Flowers

Once I gave you, wet
from moon-drenched
night fields, spray

of goldenrod

brought to your bed among
log walls.

That season changed:

stark armature of flowers, a stalk
and sharp
split pods of milkweed, now

is all I bring

from which
on fine thread flowers
in seed in

hazard blown

lie in the dark snow
beyond these
plastered walls

out there

where trees
in clumps, or singly, grow
in their dark beds

and grasses
blow in the damp wind.

David Knight

Born 1926. Teaches English at Victoria College, Toronto. Two books: *The Army Does Not Go Away* (poems) and *Farquharson's Physique and What It Did to his Mind* (a novel). Both grew out of a year's sojourn in Nigeria in 1965–66.

The Military Governors

Nigeria, January 1966

How well we mean! how good we are!
(Don't dare to disagree with us.)
To exorcise an incubus
We govern from an armoured car.

Opposed to a corrupting fuss,
We order, simplify, debar.
We are the sergeants of a star,
The drivers of the omnibus.

Our reputations cannot mar.
Nothing we do is scandalous.
Where other men are ruinous,
We are conclusive. Here we are.

We lack ambition, animus,
Or scores to settle, near or far.
No one plucks feathers from our tar.
(We burned the Northern Premier *thus!*)

Esse et Percipi

I walk in a dark living-room, having turned off
the light.
Across the street, behind a third-floor window,
I see a neighbour retreat, blue dwindling back
with white hair
Shrink below sill, having left on the light.

If she walks on a floor, it is an act of faith to
believe it;
If she has a life or a consciousness, another such
act:
How would eyes in that blank head acknowledge
a room?
I here, as part of darkness, do not have to believe
it.

I become myself dim tangible walls, floor,
doorway,
Exhale like ink in water to fill, feel, all
Corners, planes, angles. Distinct, distant, blue
Back sinks through a single yellow square,
doorway

To what? The unimaginable second life patrols
Its floorless void. We try to believe about souls.

Born 1939 in
Nelson, BC
Lived always in
interior mountain
country of
Kootenays and
Okanagan lakes of
British Columbia
wrote poetry with
brother Red Lane
until he met
Bowering and then
died and I moved
to West Coast
where I started

**Patrick
Lane**

Very Stone House
with Bissett Mayne
Brown and
magazine *Up th
tube (with one i
open)* with Chuck
Carlson. Now
moving to Hazelton
BC lost city in
great north where
I can dig into my
old pure scene of
god/people
mountains and my
own love. Books
and broadsheets:
Letters from Savage

Prospector

Old man, you prospected summer
country of caves and gold.
With the rattlesnake and spider
you were a black widow without a mate
gone deep chrome yellow—
you shared with the sun
a babble of flowers and full
brown flawless centres where
you walked in a wilderness
of golden sleep.

Once I was a child
and saw you touch a mountain
wasp with your finger
tip to wing he didn't move
but shivered gently his petal shells
of yellow and black in the wide corner
of August. You watched solitary
wasps float down sunflower fields.

Old man, I dreamed you
wandered the mountains
in spring and planted
the hills with golden flowers.
When they found you
they said you were dead
but I knew that the wasps
had planted their eggs in you
and flowers were growing
out of your sleeping eyes.

Mind (1966), *Sunflower Seeds* (1967), *Corrugated I* (1967), *For Rita in Asylum & Calgary City Jail* and *Newspaper Walls* (both 1969).

Krestova Solitaire

Sitting there among his sunflower seeds
playing solitaire and never winning
as if the cards were irrevocably stacked
against him
                    gathering slowly   shuffling
drifting paper squares of immaculate size
together with swollen brown fingers

sunflower seeds resting on his tongue
shells splurting from his lips
unnaturally as if he were filled
with eternities of flowers gone to seed

and never winning
his ankles deep in shells and eyes
not seeing cards confuse themselves
and the table shining from his arms
forever moving   laying down one card
atop the other in the unexpected rhythm
of a dream   playing solitaire
among discarded shells

Cattle Are Stupid

Cattle are stupid.
They'll die standing, waiting for men
to bring in feed. In the stiff morning
I watch the cowboys ride out.
Each pack-horse carries
two hundred pounds of hay
for the herd locked in snow
beyond Williams Lake. Clouds of white

mist roll from the horses' mouths
like lead chain borrowed from a wind.
Riders hunch in their saddles.
Before they left, they wrapped
the horse's hooves in burlap bags.
Even so, Joel said, their blood'll mark
the trail through the ice.

Cattle are stupid.
They'll die standing.
Only men and horses curse the day.
I think of the times I wanted to be
a cowboy. Now, when it could be,
they won't trust me or my skin
to make the trip. In this weather
all the cowboys are Indians, hard
in the cutting cold on the crusted lake.

Last Night in Darkness

Last night in darkness someone killed our cat.
Dipped her in gas. Set her aflame.
Her scattered kittens adorned the yard
in opaque sacks where she aborted them;
none of them burned in her pain.

As I gathered them in a paper bag
I had to pull off slugs
who'd gathered for the feast.
Their scavenger trails hovered
on her body like a mist.

Just to forget her
I leaned heavy in the morning
thrusting with my shovel

deep into earth behind the daisies
reminded only of the other
graves I'd dug

while my son prepared them
for peace. Took each one
out of their paper coffin.
Drove apple blossoms into their eyes—
even the mother who was so scarred.

Dennis Lee was born in 1939 in Toronto, where he directs the House of Anansi Press. He has written three books of poetry and edited several others.

Dennis Lee

Glad for the Wrong Reasons

Night and day it
goes on, it goes
on. I hear what feel like ponderous immaculate
lizards moving through. I call it
absence I call it silence but often I am
glad for the wrong reasons.
Many times at 6 AM there is a
fiendish din of cans, like now
for instance and we
lunge up punctured through the
blur & the broken
glass of last night's argument, fetching up
groggy on a landscape of bed, well I can
taste our dubious breath and look it's
me, babe, I wobble my neck and lounge the
trophy from my dream across your belly, your
body slouches towards me, jesus, there is
something about our lives that
doesn't make sense, tomorrow
I'll fix them up, remind me, the garbage
cans have stopped now but the room is
bright too bright to
fix I mean ah jesus I burrow slow
motion back to sleep; and the
lizards resume
their phosphorescent progress, I crowd towards
them but I should not be
here now, swallowing fast & doggedly gawking
& staying put and glad but
glad for the wrong reasons.

When It Is Over

Love, what other space are you
  going into? Under my eyes
your eyes recede; it is the gradual brunt of
  jubilation easing through
your body. So. Your body is full of listening,
  exquisite among its own
shockwaves. What
  space have you gone into?

I am the other
  music but it is not
myself you hear.
  World within world.
When it is over, love, that great
  attuned space,
do not come back and try to tell me where, for it is
  over. And I know.

400: Coming Home

You are still on the highway and the great light of
noon comes over the asphalt, the gravelled
shoulders. You are on the highway, there is a kind of
laughter, the cars pound
south. Over your shoulder the scrub-grass, the
  fences,
the fields wait patiently as though someone
believed in them. The light has laid it
upon them. One
crow scrawks. The edges
take care of themselves, there is
no strain, you can almost hear it, you
inhabit it.

Back in the city many things you lived for are
coming apart. Transistor rock still fills
back yards, in the parks young men in consort do
  things to
hondas, there will be
heat lightning, beer on the porches, goings on.
That is not it.

And you are still on the highway. There are no
houses, no farms. Across the median, past the
  swish and thud of the
northbound cars, beyond the opposite
fences, the fields, the
climbing escarpment, solitary in the
bright eye of the sun the
birches dance, and they
dance. They have
their reasons. You do not know
anything.
Cicadas call now, in the darkening swollen air
  there is dust
in your nostrils; a
kind of laughter; you are still on the highway.

Twice winner of the Governor General's Award, Dorothy Livesay was born in Winnipeg in 1909. She studied at the University of Toronto, the Sorbonne and UBC. From 1960 to 1963 she was a UNESCO specialist in Northern Rhodesia.

Dorothy Livesay

The Unquiet Bed (1967) contains her most recent love poems, together with the poem "Zambia," which grew out of her experience with UNESCO. The next year she published a selection of longer Canada-centred poems called *The Documentaries.* Dorothy Livesay was writer-in-

Dream

Sudden
a sceptred bird
swept through the window
into the blue room
and dazzled me

I think I swooned
he stooped
and pecked out my eyes
  I move in darkness now
  fumbling the walls
  trying to remember
  blue

    (I have closed the window
    and the sun falls cold
    through glass)

The Operation

1

And I too
after the blaze of being
  alive
faced the wall
over which breath must be thrown

faced the wall
scratched by the graffiti
  of trying
and made there
my trembling mark

residence at UNB
from 1966 to 1968
and is now teaching
in the Department
of English, University
of Alberta at
Edmonton.

When the knife was poised
a warm flame leaped   between us
I, victim
grateful to be saved
and he, appraising
how to create from bone and flesh
a new creature.
The needle shot into my arm
and I was his.

3

In the dazed days that followed
he used to appear
in silent white precision
at my door
and stand there till I saw him.
A nod: he waited with pursed lips
eyes quizzical beneath the furry brows
until I raged and ranted—
or docile on blue mornings
acknowledged all
solicitudes . . .
between us still
that intimate, flashing bond.

4

Now it is over! He pronounces health
I walk, near steady
out of his office, down his corridor
(the elevator sighs
the breath I fought for)
outside, pale
the autumn smog, the foul
snarl of commuting cars

and pavement's glare:
I have to breathe deep, here
to feel, in this drugged air
alive.

5

This loving was a sickness, too
in which we said farewell
so many times
and each goodbye a prelude, prescope
  of the next
swung needles deeper into flesh
  split the mind's peace.
Listen! when rain rattles the branches
  our ghost shivers.

A kind of disease between us
  love was
indulged in as excuse
  for going to bed
we transmitted kisses
and I caught between my thighs
  the antibody.

6

From my convalescent window
I see you cured
jay-walking on robson street
  a well man
    free of opposites
it's cloudy still
rain
smirches the pain

7

Morning: I face
wet pavement distorted
mirrors
    (green Christmas and your lean body
    lounging along the shore
    your lunging arms
    flung against boulders)
I decide to complete the operation
tear myself into four quarters
scatter the pieces
North:
    a crystal city of ice
    arching up, stretching out daily
    dazedly
    into uncoiling
    animal sun—
    another kingdom.

8

Until I'd found a doorway
I could stand in, push against
I did not know how shrunk
I had become
for now the *he*, the *you*, are one
and gone
and I must measure me.
O let me grow and push
upright!
ever aware of height
and the cry
to reach a dazzled strangeness:
sun-pierced sky.

Born 1922. Went to McGill and the University of Toronto. Librarian, Massey College and Professor of English, University College, Toronto. Books: *The Heart is Fire* (1959), *It Is All Around* (1960), *Poet Talking* (1964), *A &B &C & . . .* and *Millwood Road Poems* (both 1969).

Douglas Lochhead

Into the Swamp

The mad shallows
at turtle dawn:
the darting time,
the canoe slips
on the water top
and I glide it
so close underneath
to shadowy schools,
sand clouds in
underwater piles
and the shadows grow
into thin light
in the waveless place
and what the swamp
echoes bring are
heron, bittern
and the long hidden
fight prolonged
going on
just underneath.

Canadian Jollies

LOUIE

I

Bear-happy, squaw-loose Louie
in a big winter wind,
authentic life in a clearing,
like sweat and foot foot
through the stiff north he knew
running once, walking

crossed himself before thoughts.
Do I care who is in the snare?
Do I club the beggar in the trap,
or does he club me?
It is too cold to ask. I whack
the beggars when they move.

Bear-happy humpy Louie
this blast, this cold, is all yours Louie.

2

I bolts the door and licks
my scrapes, my toes they thaw
between her thighs   my squaw
she is fourteen   scratch

Who knows what her lone wait for Louie is?
What ding dong does in this old shack
my pot-bellied warmth & her hard
charms endure the night, outlast the storm.

Breed, breed the wild dream says
our priest dances with a mini,
my squabble in heaven
will play real hell with the harps.
That's me, Louie.

3

O my whisky Louie, trapper of bears,
windy lover, snow stomper, squaw chaser,
we met this zero-cracking day,
north of Wascasu.
Someone had hiccups eating sausages.
You kissed your squaw,
and what could she do then,
but take the winter draughts,

and wash your drawers?
The big man-toss talk and drink we had Louie,
and your lies and mine about life-love
stood high as the quick, green, polar shafts of light.
O my whisky Louie, trapper of bears, windy lover,
up there, north of Wascasu.

ETIENNE

Etienne Brûlé—what in hell happened?
I can only ask your ghost, take him out,
drink wine in some private smoke-pit.
What in hell up there? What in hell down there?
". . . probably the first white man . . . to see
lakes Huron, Ontario, Superior and Erie
. . . murdered by the Hurons, June 1633."

"he left no personal description. . . ." He
shoved off, like Rimbaud maybe?
Etienne into the woods, traded to the Algonquin
  chief,
you became interpreter (truchement)
walking Huron dictionary. First one,
you heller, to shoot Sault-Saint-Louis;
first one to take the torture
from the Iroquois. Did you,
did you not talk miracles when a storm
threw bullets on your enemy?
But no wonder with all that torture, white water,
you were, they say, ". . . vicious and much addicted
to women." Okay for that
but what in hell out there—they eat you
after you were twenty years a brother.
It was the Bear Tribe of the Hurons.
The woman scholar who writes your battered
  story
puts in all the details, all the bones
she can find.

I was born in Toronto in 1941. Novels: *Julian the Magician* (1963), *The Twelve Circles of the Night* (1970). Poetry: *The Rising Fire* (1963), *Breakfast for Barbarians* (1966), *The Shadow-Maker* (1969). Am now translating a modern Arabic novel.

Gwendolyn MacEwen

The Film

I think I must have been with you
in all the movie-houses of the world,
or else you perform
in the dark theatres of my blood
parts you never meant to play;
  did you watch too long
those Universal spectacles
of wars where nobody ever dies,
of monstrous lovers who kiss forever
  down the corridors
of Time?
The fervent curtains fall apart
and the silver screen is skin.

I think the walls of the place you live in
whisper names and legends in the night,
and wispy film unwinds, unwinds
in some unseen projector run
by a cruel Technician who merely wants
  to drive you blind,
and send his Cast of Thousands
clanging through your sleep.

I think that when you raise your hand
against those walls
your flesh becomes a screen,
  the drama unfolds
along your fingers
and across your open palm the armies run
and down your veins their false blood falls;
  I want to tell you—
Look this is the kind of war nobody needs,
these are the kisses meant to kill.
But now the images have claimed your face,
  you are alive with lies and legends,
the silver reel unravels in your skull,
the dark film roars forever through your blood.

Born Barnston, Que., 1935. Went to Mount Allison University and McGill. Now living near Kingston. A book of poems, *The Welder's Arc*, was published by Quarry Press in 1969.

Stuart MacKinnon

Song in a Rainy Season

See the rain come down
Like a ton on the factitious
Back of upland.

Likely in a lifetime
A ton of water falls
On each man's back,
Carried unnoticed over
Backbone and asscrack.

The roof heaves
Its accumulation
Into the drain,
That hardened artery
Of certainty.

Lying on my bed
The eaves for ears
Let the weight fall
On my hands.

Only hands can measure
The shift and sway
And the cruel accumulation.

Let the rain fall
On my hands as I lie
Back to back
With the sudden earth.

My Grandfather / the Thunderer

My Grandfather retired to a wooden
house down in the village
where the sun never set
and there were large maple trees
to the west side. He lived
there alone for twenty years
belching to the hollow house
and eating Aylmer's tomato soup.
Alone except for thunderstorms
when his hearing aid began
to crackle, and he bellowed
his responsive shouting matches
with Zeus, until a close clap
sent him fumbling for the
volume control. Lived alone
with hollow ears in a booming shade.

Professor of English at York University, Eli Mandel won a Governor General's Award in 1967 for his book of poems, *An Idiot Joy.*

Lake Wabamum

Eli Mandel

and all the limp, incurious men
my compatriots
                    teachers, poets
clerics
        when poems flicker
behind their eyeballs
like the aura epileptics
say they see unbidden
bending like poplars
at the whisper of thunder
rumouring students
rifling private secret files

trouble themselves like wavelets
thrown by a casual craft's
turbulence moving
                    small
pebbles only
a savage one dark summer
sifted in idle augury

look a last time
at frogmen and gilas
their webbed hands

reflect
        amphibious
monsters, children
ransack your cities
taught this alien
reckless spasm
neither you nor I
polite summarists
knew poems convulsed

Wabamum: Gulls Feeding

will no one rid me of this parliament
of foul
          gulls
                    that even the evening
deafens
          until it too lies
athwart icelandic clouds
as if stunned by Eric the Red
who with one blade
                              lit those fires
distant and signalling trees?

Tiny as balloonists or stars
the partial seeds parachute
from a maze of Russian poplars.

The air
thridden with harmonious motes
hums and hums again.
                                        Red Guards
singing in their cells?
                                   Demos?
And the gulls insatiable.

Tom Marshall

Tom Marshall was born at Niagara Falls, Ont. in 1938. As a child he lived for several years in the southern United States, but returned to Canada in 1944. He was educated at Queen's University, where he is now an Assistant Professor of English. His first book of poems, *The Silences of Fire*, was published in 1969. He is also the author of *The Psychic Mariner*, a book on the poems of D. H. Lawrence published in 1970, and a book on the poems of A. M. Klein. He is editor of *Quarry* and head of the Quarry Press.

Space-Age

London, 10 June 1968

Like jacks thrown against the sky
the jets scatter. America burns
her paranoid landscape.
England clucks while news is hot.
Another of the people's tribunes is shot.

The Return

It is good to be back
in Canada where things
are so intensely themselves.

The grass, the colour of the
shadow of the grass.
September light separates things

carefully. Trees, clouds, blades
of grass are bathed
in it, cleansed. Waves lift

and ripen in the crackling
air. The brown
pools untouched by wind

in the hollows of large
protruding roots shine
secretly in the park.

Born 1944 in Montreal. Has lived on the West Coast since 1965. Books and broadsheets: *That Monocycle the Moon* (1964), *Tiptoeing on the Mount* (1965), *From the Portals of Mouseholes* (1966), *ticklish ticlicorice, the gigolo teaspoon, earseed, Anewd, Manimals* and *mutetations* (1969).

Seymour Mayne

For NPL

From the strange sunbleak
  landscape of the Okanagan
you came with the grownup
  innocent longings,
with stories I could never
  muster of teeming Montreal.
Rattlesnake dens, scorpions,
  the black widow
of my fearful city imagination.
  now simple
totems of your words.
They destroy no-one.
  Almost everyone survives
in that open Interior.
  And if they die—
it was just another thing
  with the hazy cold,
the breaking clay cliffs,
  the rotting fruit,
the sparse grass,
  and the scattered rusted tools,
relics of earlier struggles.

Night moist,
coast lights glitter coldly.
Patrol car hums close,
razes the beachhead,
a wide searching thrust
heavy like a falling beam.

Hidden, halfburied
by this barkgouged log
we heave—
            wind rush unbidden

calling on,
rising from clash
the piercing shrillness!

Bared belly breaking
gasps drown
in sea sound.
Low-flung waves
rise out,
arch
and shatter.

1947

Six mounted child-photos
tilt one from the other
in the eggshell frame
under glass
as if frozen in statue tag

Curls falling
over the small ears
the child holds for himself alone
in chubby hands
the ball of many bands
Shiny booties hide
the impatient tiny toes
as they may have wriggled

That smile in bubble cheeks
—did it keep the photographer
at bay with memories then?
Did he have a child
who had fallen for a stray bouncing ball,
the lurching screeching once

again holding him off
as he snapped it then?

For that flashbulb
bursting in a sharp kiss
tore
on that last photo
that bite of whiteness
from my cheek
twenty years ago

Born London, England, 1930. Very Irish Dad. Came to Canada 1956. Number of odd and execrable jobs rivals Newlove's list, includes worm-picking. *Smoking the City* (1965). Poems and reviews in usual mags. Wrote long prose work *The Bad Book*: Ralph Maud's editorial labours on this now reaching conclusion.

Bryan McCarthy

50 Miles North of Montreal

for Edie

I crunch
up the path
into the snow-
crusted farmhouse

The flutter
of the oil-stove
flame is
delicate, three-
        dimensional
in the room. . . .
I stare
at a leaf
for half an hour
without guilt. It
intrigues me
strangely.
I stare at a
tilted post outside
motionless wheel atop
for a clothesline,
        gaunt
totem-pole in this
lonely land. . . .
Marvellous . . . leaves
in the room . . . forests
entering the mind. . . .

I get up, open
a creaking door
        slowly (smooth
        creak saw-
toothed creak) close it and
open it
listening

Then you come in
suddenly
real, face
flushed
        eyes wet-bright
from freezing air
laughing
stamping snow from boots

and behind you the brilliant
day
  is opening out—
with its lakes, its trees
and its marvellous
nameless spaces.

A few words about my dearly beloved self

I turned my back
    angrily
        on bryan mccarthy

strode
    into a forest
        of abandoned postures

saw marble
        fists of my
        lost selves
clenched against the sky

touched enigmatic lettering

        on indecipherable
            pedestals

I yelled out to the Age
and heard
a nineteenth-century echo

in the marble forest

Lugging an antique
angst
I
dragged myself into
twentieth-century
imagery

Existed
as a precarious edge
of verbal brilliance
on a plane of black ice
machined
to a millionth of an inch

by an inscrutable process

A billion words hammered
Nothingness
into my head

Reality was
annihilated
with a pun

subjectivity
with a quip

my life became a remote legend
the lies that
I perfected with grandiose
eloquence

became my prized reality

If I lived, if I begat
children it was done
out of the corner of my eye

while staring at a steel
icon

And thus
I cultivated a secret
insouciance

I screwed the moon for monocle
into my eye

saw, in its chilly light,
two-dimensional men
jigging

I gathered my abandoned angers
I steeled myself

I cleft my way
through a sea
of shrugged shoulders

a grinning
death-ship.

Purdy's Place

Roblin Lake, Ontario

At night the
windows are
black
mirrors

slither
        shrink
            bulge
and collapse
            and I would yell
HEY YOU OLD SOD
but am just a wee
bit spooked. . . .

There is nothing outside. No
thing. This is Purdy's place.
The lake is a preposterous
hypothesis not to be
countenanced.
The telephone mainlines
to God
but the switchboard's
burnt out; no matter,
with a curious, jerking
movement of
my right hand
I produce a dozen poems.
    Purdy sleeps
gasps
behind a screen: there, a pale
blue sun illumines the country
of our defeat; he lumbers alone

leaving a trail of bones
which no-one not in a million
ages, will discover. . . .

It gets cold. Night's
slabbed against the creaking
A-frame house, close
and comforting. My lips
are locked securely
into my skull

but there's much, much yet
good friends in the solip-
sistic fridge, much
wire to
bite upon, sweet air
to chew good friends,
before the slow mendacious frost
cracks in.

It gets
colder. I hoard
myself like a spark
in a lump of blue ice,
plot diabol-
ically a bristling
electrical dangerous past to be
tossed, sputtering
into the cosmos. . . .

It gets cold
indeed. The giant
behind his screen
is gasping, groping:

And over our heads
the lean
prayerful rafters
parody a discarded myth.

Art's Variety

A poem should touch the hearer with a sense of his own weakness, and should institute some comparison between mankind and flowers

—E. M. Forster

She was so small and pretty
my heart broke, and breaking
tried to determine her age.
I wondered if she wore a bra
then dimly picked out the straps.

I bought toothpaste, fuses
and a twin-pack of lightbulbs
and she said: "Are you sure
there's two bulbs in there?"
Then opened the pack to check.
"I'd hate to have you go home . . .
and find yourself with one bulb."

"She's somewhere between 12 and 30,"
I thought, amazed at the delicate
fences around her, the tiny bones
and features, the fleshy moat
and her age so indeterminable
like a tiny tree suspended upside-down
deep in the centre of her brain.

I was born in Hamilton in 1940 and am a life-long resident of Hamilton's east end. I'm employed as a proofreader with the *Spectator*. Recent books include *The Poem Poem* (1967), *The Saladmaker* (1968), *Letters from the Earth to the Earth* (1969) and *The Great Canadian Sonnet* (1970).

David McFadden

Le sommeil est plein de miracles!

Don't go mistaking paradise for that home across the road

—Bob Dylan

I know what I remember having seen
in dreams was not seen at all,
but the memory distorts and makes seem
visual those miraculous messages from the blue

so that I remember having seen things
that not only would be impossible in existence
but also impossible to depict graphically.

One dream had me flipping through an album
containing photos of all the future Buddhas
and if I was Picasso I couldn't give any hints
of the ecstatic fullness of those faces.

In fact what I saw in those faces
isn't expressible in a human face
so what was it that happened?

What part of heaven did I glimpse
that was so beyond my sensual life
I could only remember it in a metaphor
of flipping through an album of pictures?

A question for dream scientists of the future?
And once I woke up full of enlightenment,
I was the oldest and wisest of the immortals

and babbling gibberish. I'd been standing
on the sidewalk looking up at a marquee
on which in about nine words was given
the complete raison d'être of space and time

and later, shaving in the bathroom
felt as foolish as a bull with tits
because those nine words had become none.

Every night in sleep I touch the key
of the Gods, and float through endless sky
and all day long I'm thinking, thinking.

Kenneth McRobbie

Born 1929. Here represented by three previously unpublished poems from a sequence "The Prairie Smokes." Has published *Eyes Without a Face*, appeared in *Poetry of Mid-Century* and is bringing out translations of the work of the Hungarian poet Ferenc Juhász, *The Boy Changed into a Stag*. A new volume of his verse will appear soon. Came to Canada in 1954 from England, is a Canadian citizen, teaches cultural history at the University of Manitoba, edits *Mosaic*.

The Prairie Smokes

I: GENERATION

This at least we can still believe:
  —what is on fire is happening.

So we wait,
          in the long winter's night
that burns invisibly upon our faces,

for a view of the flames we heard about,
  though smoke-shrouded from the start,
not even a glimmer on the underside of the clouds.

How long has it been? Just for this,
  a tall monument of cold smoke,
white as a negative, rising from the earth
into space ever blacker yet more visible
  like something left behind there

that revolves, rolling shadowed segments over
and slowly in again upon each other.

  There are enough of us not to care
for such a mere sign of sustained seeming life,
mere presence upon this circumference of absence.

  Everything else has grown older with us.
Our eyes stream in the cold air
bringing the smart of distant smoke

—strain, and tire of its shifting principle
of mysteries enveloping each inaccessible
  suspected centre.

  Not lightning striking, or
the blast from some ascending blackened nozzle
sent up this permanent, pale smoke
  in our incombustible place.

This fire was set. So
to show respect
—the death of fire is also an event—
it must not just happen to go out
in a rain shower, or through lack of fuel,
when it can be kicked to pieces.

II: FAR SMOKE

Nothing else in sight all day
but the far smokes shaping the light
moving, but never nearer
as if the earth is returning
all it has left of the night,

rising slowly from the prairie's rim
like black trees or wing-flutter,
and on the wind
vibrations of distant sounds
that have already come to an end.

Something is happening overhead,
at the corner of vision, just over
the horizon, never
attracting attention here, before
somewhere else reaching a conclusion.

Prairie smokes do not burn or explode.
They drift and reform like memories
of what was unfulfilled,
safely loved ghosts or flowers of an
invisible therefore no purpose.

In the smoke surface is projected
to the highest power of generalization
against the sky's screen,
without responsibility, without dimension
except eternity's, that nothing.

Against light,
  destroyer
 of worlds,

innocence
  rises
 from the plain,

curved, smooth,
  straining
 out of plane.

Its distance,
  creation
 of the dark,

looses
  our feet
 of light.

Born in Saskatchewan in 1938, now living in British Columbia. *Black Night Window* published in 1968, *The Cave* in 1970.

John Newlove

Man Drift

The
men drift
in space like
incompetent fish far

above any
spike-
y unseen trees; far
above the brown earth shift

metals, ceramics, plastics,
floating at incredible
speeds; tricks
and technical garbage

blink
in light bounces;
space is vast, inaudible,
we are small,

we shrink
to weighing ounces,
quickly age;
we leave our

excrement behind,
and that of all
our machines as a
remind-

er to us that
we can sail away
from the mar-
red earth, the flat
earth. Some being
must know.
Is God seeing
what we show?—

dolphins do not,
nor dogs, our simpering pets,
not the hot
white wandering polar

bear,
which sets
its eyes to the track
beneath it, not the solar

one, roaming on and back
in the live snow
that meets him where-
ever he shall go.

Dream

The luxurious trembling sea, winding atmosphere
of thick death and life, egg-filled, swarming
and empty,

rides on unknown rock and infested slabs of slime
epochs deep in flesh that has no memories,

no interest except to live, survive, shambling
through cold currents, only occasionally
breaking the shining opaque lid of the wet
universe,

a touch of animal foam on the surface among the
few floating twigs that drift away from the
deserted earth. . . .

And the red and brown vine-tangled land is empty
except for armoured insects lugging their
invaluable trophies back and forth,

dry matted grass feet deep whipped in the wind,
rotten fallen trees, crisp shards of leaves,

shifting deserts of sand and bare plains strewn
with rocks like ankle bones stretching across
the sterile continents, dust in the stark air,

no movement except that of ants and beetles and the
great swaying wooden vegetables, dead. . . .

The sea moves nervously, through it strange beasts
search for food, unthinkingly constant in their
paths,

the earth rustles dryly and in the bright sky the
stars continue to shine,

and the great galaxial wheel rolls smoothly in its
unhuman silence that contains all sounds. . . .

The ice will return again, and life and then the
fire too. . . .

Dream 3

Bees won't fly when it's this cold;
sixty degrees is what they need.

Wings freeze. A hundred miles beyond
the white frontier the European honey bee

frightens the natives. They know it;
it moves ahead. Wings freeze, though.

In winter one Indian
moves slowly through the snow,
hoping for honey, a taste.

Dream 4

The lone figure leans in the snow.
a rifle is stuck beside him:
one hand is on it.

He waits an approaching figure.
He will decide, when it comes,
to kill or to run.

It is the white centre
of the world he squats in.

Alden Nowlan

Alden Nowlan, 37, is the author of seven books of poetry, one of which, *Bread, Wine and Salt*, won the Governor General's Award for Poetry. He has been awarded two Canada Council grants and in 1967 went to Ireland and England on a Guggenheim Fellowship. A selection of his short stories, *Miracle at Indian River*, was published in 1968. He writes a weekly column for the Saint John *Telegraph-Journal*, of which he was formerly night news editor. He is currently writer in residence at UNB.

The Waiter's Smile

The waiter in the Admiral Beatty
smiles as he apologizes
for not being permitted to sell me
an ounce and a half of rum because, alas sir,
I am not wearing
a four-in-hand necktie.
It is a sweet smile
and there is a little movement of the head
that goes with it and a certain sadness in the eyes
—all waiters have perfected it.
And I bet the privilege
of giving that smile once a night
is rated almost as high
as a five-dollar tip.
You see, he's telling me,
Listen, Boob, there's some things
your filthy money can't buy
and one of them is good breeding, say I,
who am keeper of public decorum;
and no matter how many times I call you "Sir,"
you know, and I know,
who's top dog in this game.

Roots

I've seen only one picture of my great-grandfather.
He was pointed out to me
as the fourth man from the left in a photograph
of about thirty men and two teams of horses
posed in front of a logging camp in the 1880s.
You find the same kind of picture
in histories of the west, a posse

come back with the bodies, they used to prop up
the dead
with their eyes still open and pretend
to be holding them at gunpoint.
And I seem to remember
similar pictures of the Serbian army
during the First World War, my great-grandfather
even wore a sort of Slavic blouse
and the same kind of moustache.
There are also pictures
of white men after a lynching.
Nobody is smiling
because these were time-exposures
and if you must keep your face still
it's safest and simplest
to shut your mouth, although best
not to clench your teeth because then
you may start to imagine
you're smothering, take a deep breath
and spoil everything,
and their eyes are black slits
because it's impossible
to keep from blinking once you try not to.
Though I don't believe they'd have smiled
even if that had been mechanically possible.
It was a ritual then, this picture-taking,
the photographer down from Halifax,
a city man in a linen collar and a derby hat,
who put a black hood over his head and sometimes
set off an explosion at the crucial moment.
They knew
this was an instant
that could be held
against them.
So they look very tough and their hands are free
or grip peaveys or axes.
I get the feeling
my great-grandfather is trying to convince
somebody
he'd use that axe on a man, if he had to.

He holds it the way those Serbs held their rifles.
And I have no doubt
he'd have joined a manhunt
or helped with a lynching,
would have thought it unmanly
to have done otherwise.
Or maybe it's only
that he's proud of the axe,
maybe he was an axeman like his grandson, my
father,
who could make the tallest tree
fall where he wanted it, aim its tip at a spot
no bigger than a fig
of chewing tobacco, and hit it.
I read the histories of countries
and his time seems like yesterday
but because he was human
and my own, he seems so old
as to almost stand
outside of time.
It amazes me, thinking:
he must have been at least fifteen years
younger than I am that day the winter sun
lapped up and locked into a small black box
an infinitesimal portion of his soul.

Michael Ondaatje

Born in Ceylon in 1943, Michael Ondaatje has lived in Canada since 1962. His poems have appeared in *New Wave Canada, The Penguin Book of Canadian Verse* and *The Oxford Book of Modern Canadian Verse.* Books: *The Dainty Monsters* (1967), *The Man with Seven Toes* (1969), *The Collected Works of Billy the Kid* (1970).

Kim, at half an inch

Brain is numbed
is body touch
and smell, warped light

Hooked so close
her left eye
is only a golden blur
her ear / a vast
musical instrument of flesh

The moon spills off my shoulder
slides into her face

Gold and black

At night the gold and black slashed bees come
pluck my head away. Vague thousands drift
leave brain naked stark as liver
each one carries atoms of flesh, they
walk my body in their fingers.
The mind stinks out.

In the black Kim is turning
a geiger counter to this pillow.
She cracks me open like a lightbulb.

Love, the real,
will terrify
the dreamer in his riot cell.

King Kong meets Wallace Stevens

Take two photographs—
Wallace Stevens and King Kong
(Is it significant that I eat bananas as I write this?)

Stevens is portly, benign, a white brush cut
striped tie. Businessman but
for the dark thick hands, the naked brain,
the thought in him.

Kong is staggering
lost in New York streets again
a spawn of annoyed cars at his toes.
The mind is nowhere.
Fingers are plastic, electric under the skin.
He's at the call of Metro-Goldwyn-Mayer.

Meanwhile W. S. in his suit
is thinking chaos is thinking fences.
In his head the seeds of fresh pain,
his exorcising,
the bellow of locked blood
golden fear and dying.

The hands drain from his jacket
pose in the murderer's shadow.

Notes for the legend of Salad Woman

Since my wife was born
she must have eaten
the equivalent of two-thirds
of the original garden of Eden.
Not the dripping lush fruit
or the meat in the ribs of animals
but the green salad gardens of that place.
The arena of green
would have been eradicated
as if the right filter had been removed
leaving only the skeleton of coarse brightness.

All green ends up eventually
churning in her left cheek.
Her mouth is a laundromat of spinning drowning
herbs.
She is never in fields
but is sucking the pith out of grass.
I have noticed the very leaves from flower
decorations
grow sparse in their week-long performance in
our house.
The garden is a dust bowl.

On our last day in Eden
as we walked out
she nibbled the leaves
at her breasts and crotch.

Mmm but there's none to touch
none to equal
the Chlorophyl Kiss.

P. K. Page was born in 1916. Her poetry first appeared in *Unit of Five* (1944). Her books include *As Ten as Twenty* (1946), *The Metal and the Flower* (winner of the Governor General's Award in 1954) and *Cry Ararat* (1968).

P. K. Page

Fly: on Webs

There are two kinds of web: the one
not there. A sheet of glass.
Look! I am flying through air,
spinning in emptiness . . . SPUNG!
. . . bounced on a flexible wire,
caught in invisible guys.

The other a filigree, gold
as the call of a trumpet, a sun
to my myriad-facetted eye.
A season. A climate. Compelled
and singing hosannas I fly:
I dazzle, I struggle. I drown.

A Backwards Journey

When I was a child of say, seven,
I still had serious attention to give
to everyday objects. The Dutch Cleanser—
which was the kind my mother bought—
in those days came in a round container
of yellow cardboard around which ran
the very busy Dutch Cleanser woman
her face hidden behind her bonnet
holding a yellow Dutch Cleanser can
on which a smaller Dutch Cleanser woman
was holding a smaller Dutch Cleanser can
on which a minute Dutch Cleanser woman
held an imagined Dutch Cleanser can. . . .

This was no game. The woman led me
backwards through the eye of the mind
until she was the smallest point
my thought could hold to. And at that moment
I think I knew that if no one called
and nothing broke the delicate jet
of my attention, that tiny image
could smash the "atom" of space and time.

Knitter's Prayer

Unknit me—
all those blistering strange small intricate stitches—
shell stitch, moss stitch, pearl and all too plain;
unknit me to the very first row of ribbing,
let only the original simple knot remain.

Then let us start again.

Another Space

Those people in a circle on the sand
are dark against its gold
turn like a wheel
revolving in a horizontal plane
whose axis—do I dream it?—
vertical
invisible
immeasurably tall
rotates a starry spool.

Yet *if* I dream
why in the name of heaven are fixed parts
within me set in motion
like a poem?

Those people in a circle reel me in.
Down the whole length of golden beach I come
willingly pulled by their rotation
slow
as a moon pulls waters
on a string
their turning circle winds around its rim.

I see them there in three dimensions yet
their height implies another space
their clothes'
surprising chiaroscuro postulates
a different spectrum.
What kaleidoscope
does air construct
that all their movements make a compass rose
surging and altering?
I speculate
on some dimension I can barely guess.

Nearer I see them dark-skinned.
They are dark. And beautiful.
Great human sunflowers spinning in a ring
cosmic as any bumble-top
the vast
procession of the planets in their dance.
And nearer still I see them—"a Chagall"—
each fiddling on an instrument—its strings
of some black woollen fibre
and its bow—feathered—
an arrow almost.
Arrow *is.*

For now the headman—one step forward—shoots
(or does he bow or does he lift a kite

up and over the bright pale dunes of air?)
to strike the absolute centre of my skull
my absolute centre somehow
with such skill
such staggering lightness
that the blow is love.

And something in me melts.
It is as if a glass partition melts—
or something I had always thought was glass—
some pane that halved my heart
is proved, in its melting, ice.

And to-fro all the atoms pass
in bright osmosis
hitherto
in stasis locked
where now a new
direction opens like an eye.

Three Crosses

Outside the traffic ties itself in ribbons.
Neon green eyes on wooden models beckon come.
Bloodshot red the traffic stops.
Music from a tavern,
syrup from a street-corner soul;
everywhere the smell, the sugar, the smoke—
the city dotting the landscape,
a maple-syrup pot.

Morning.
Sunlight splashes in the window
drops of light bouncing from the snow;
Carolyn in bed tired
after a night of hustling
a day of working.

Her stockings are still on
legs like logs
jammed in a river.
She feels her legs.
No one stole her money.
Her few thefts she calls income tax.
She runs to the bathroom,
splashes water,
hides her hair under a wig.
She powders her delicate long nose,
puts shadows to erase shadows from her eyes.
She looks in the mirror half pleased—
her nose a stick,
two eyes, arms of a cross.
Every morning she pays off.
Money in the bank
and she knows why.

Mavis saves her money in church.
She sits waiting for consolation.
The priest comes walking down the hill—

I teach school when I can't afford to sit down and write poetry —but I like teaching school. I work under one title, "Energy equals Mercy Squared." I have coined the word "wheachery," which comes from the words "healer" and "teacher." I live in Toronto.

Mervyn Procope

a slight grade;
the steeple cross fleshed to make a lover's face. . . .
  It was a marriage into an old family. . . .
This morning he loves behind curtains of a
  disappearing face.
Today the words can't come
like sap from lips.
The singing bird of flesh is chanting
through corridors of china-shop bodies,
marking off territories in blood.
Mavis left her panties on the floor
like a piece of soft white feather.

Three weeks he carried it in his pocket.
Three weeks he rationalized:
this must be a piece of smelling meat on me,
this must be a jewel.

Bruised by the nailed cross of birth
planted in the groin,
he crept from his empty bed Golgotha
climbing to hang the panties from the steeple.

His parishioners got angry,
his board of governors tried to dismiss him.
He kept his job by saying,
he was preaching sex next Sunday.

Came the appointed Sunday,
first time in months his church was filled.
Some say it was his best sermon.
Afterwards, in theory, he was climbing
to take down his banner.
He jumped
spilling blood on Sunday people.

Such things can't happen now—
the church is too liberal.
The neon lights are green.
Carolyn is in the sportscar.
Mavis is walking.

Besides working on a poem series I am at present reworking a novel. Collections of poems have been published by Fiddlehead Books, the Ryerson Press, Emblem Books. Passing back and forth across the border, I have found that my starchy English-Canadian inheritance doesn't belong strictly anywhere, but is a framework from which to extend my living and outlook. I was born in Fredericton in 1906.

Dorothy Roberts

Float

Water goes in and out of the reed's cell,
in and out of the gill
but the boat is that form that floats.

Watertight, caulked it coerces the water to be
with it—
"Always when I am alive you are with me,
yet enter not and the lapping is continual."
This is the most graceful elaboration of the
communion,
oars dip and the ripples of progress circle about it
and the furrow behind is a form.

Go lonely boat and be at dawn in the mist
and be at evening on the beach
just out of reach of the long ripple, a shell.

Landscape

Canada grows out of its deeps now
and the snow burns off in the glow
and the snow is make-believe on the vast stretches
between
but make-believe enough to fill a child of the past
with shivers and cold love
passing at night over the rail that may leave no
track
through the wooded and white land of the broken
birch
and pine and spruce locked down and the quietness
sheeting by peculiarly to itself yet lasting so long
that it is there travelling too, a ghostly companion.

This Canada cold and huge is at the window
of the calm train all night but for the breakthrough
of occasional place, far-spaced, while its stride is
unbroken,
cold land, cold conditioning for thousands of its
children of the remote past—
so that time seems to them—
in their burial places here and there to the top of
the tombstone
or as the traveller returned breathing the warm air
against the window of cold and the sliding
companion
that does not even breathe for the crystalline
silence
waylaying one for hour on hour in tree shape and
snowdrift.

Swimmer

There being nothing closer to place itself upon
the shadow is plunged way down to the sea below
and swims there rapidly, a winged small fish in
the blue swell.

It is enlarged in its fall but we can only see it
small like a fish in the great basin of the ocean.
It is frisky with waves, sportive yet never stays
behind.

Attached to our element at such a distance
it has its own existence, it is lively and resistant
to disturbances in the waves, coming out of them
again
alive and running on with us as long as we can fly

in the bright sun above the beautiful swell of
 waters down below
the turquoise and amethyst and sheer blue ocean
and we are reassured that it can swim.

Staying

Islands are sand and shrubbery and sedge grass
willing to go, if need be, with the river,
float like a boat, or wear away while tethered
by roots of sand and rock, bound round with
 lilies.

They are the limit to which land loves the water,
paddles and deep fish move and the sandpipers
sprinkled upon it liven the sand with the heron,
clams scrawl over textured sandridges.

Dipped in the beds of lilies paddles brush quiet,
herons flap up and all is like a painting
by chinese water colourists, indeed it is one
so long and quietly these islands have persisted.

So it is logical to say that islands
coerce the things in flux to stay awhile,
to stand awhile delayed in forms and fragrances
freshening out of the mist of early morning.

Head of the
Department of
English at Althouse
College, University
of Western
Ontario. 41 years
old.

John Smallbridge

Hearing F. R. Leavis Stutter

Sibilance and stutter had settled on his speech like
shine
On polished agate, forming a shimmering design:
Vicissitude of sound became a repetitious ghost
Of parasitic light confined by the limits of its host,
That shifted, rooted, mirrored and bloomed upon
itself.

The self-same day I found it happening to myself.
My thoughts, as lightning, broke, branched and
broke,
And all prismatic brilliance was quick spent
Unvoiced by any sweet thunder,
Or even imitative stutter . . . less relevant
Than criticisms in a book of 1926 or seven.

Stutter, as thunder, geigers hidden metal;
As light, hits, reflects the coloured gem;
And stammer seems man's simplest poetry,
The hammered ring, the setting for the precious
stone.
And even all the pauses in Leavis' stutterings
Become rifts filled full with ore, or
Soundings of still deeper, darker levels.

Then he or I, each in his essential need,
What have we in speech revealed, refined?
Or have we merely bared effects ironical?

"Those who care about it can only go on caring."

Raymond Souster was born, raised, schooled and now works as a bank accountant in Toronto, this all having started in 1921. His books of verse in print are: *The Colour of the Times* (1964), *Ten Elephants on Yonge Street* (1965), *As Is* (1967), *Lost & Found* (1968)

Yeah Tigers

When our boy, Al Kaline, tagged that slider of
Washburn's
in the third today, tagged it good, sent it sailing
high and deep in the Tigers' upper deck—

Wilf, I heard that yelp of yours
clear across this crummy town,
over TV bedlam, traffic, everything—

even if it only came out
as the slightest half-whisper
from your cancer-bugged throat.

Raymond Souster

Queen Anne's Lace

It's a kind of flower
that if you didn't know it
you'd pass by the rest of your life.

But once it's pointed out
you'll look for it always,
even in places
where you know it can't possibly be.

You will never tire
of bending over to examine,
to marvel at this,
the shyest filigree of wonder
born among grasses.

You will imagine poems
as brief, as spare,
so natural with themselves
as to take breath away.

and *So Far So Good* (1969). A new volume titled *The Years* will be published in 1971. He has also acted as co-editor of: *Shapes & Sounds*, *Made in Canada*, *Generation Now* and *A & B & C &*. He won the Governor General's Award in 1964.

The Cloud

Why does my mind keep returning
to the long morning
staring at the wall
the cloudless morning when nobody worked
when nobody talked or nobody heard them
a day without pity or anger
alone with the one thought
we did that

Why do my thoughts keep to the one track?
What are they trying to hide?
Why do they always go back
to Hiroshima?

Francis Sparshott

Born (1926) and educated in England. Has taught philosophy at the University of Toronto since 1950 and written poetry since 1942. Poetry: *A Divided Voice* (1965) and *A Cardboard Garage* (1969). Most recent prose: *The Concept of Criticism* (1967).

Combermere's Mill

Combermere's mill stands over slates
on a corner in Delce. Combermere is not grinding.
To the north, allotments begin, sustained out of
tarred shacks,
framed in brass bedstead-ends, yielding starved
cabbages
for desolate pensioners. All day, and all yesterday,
the gale blew straight from the northwest, but
Combermere
is not grinding. He sits in the doorway and reads,
in his mill's shelter reads yesterday's paper, the
sweeps
sideways to the wind. Nobody comes near him.

On the ridge of the next hill, on an empty field
marked out for football, chalk under thin loam,

the soldiers prepare. One brushes mud from his
greatcoat,
most squat and say nothing. In an iron pot
on a good fire, one prepares soup. There is cabbage
in it. The tarred wood
makes a red flame. The weapons are piled.
Someone points to the mill
on the next ridge, where the smoke of their supper
whips past the idle sweeps and does not turn them.

Before the Lecture

Unknown faces
wait for my words.
What if I have no words for them?
Silence, I shall tell them, is better.

—Unimpressed faces.
"What words would you like?"
"Your words. What have you got?"
"No words you don't have already."
"But we came all this way and we spent all this
money
and we were promised words.
Give us your words."

"What use is a word without a man behind it?"
"We want words."
"There are too many words about altogether,
it is wicked to add to them. Better we should take
a pill
or pull sleeves over our heads. Things went better
when there was more desolation."
"In a general way
we would agree. But now, specifically,

here in this hall, we presently insist
upon words."

Unsympathetic faces
hiding behind bored sockets
such separate silences
as cannot be broken by
words.

Peter Stevens

I was born in 1927 and came to Canada in 1957. Poems have appeared in *To Every Thing There Is a Season, The New Romans, Best Poems of 1967* (Pacific Books) and *Fifteen Winds.* Edited a collection of critical essays, *The McGill Movement.* First book (poems): *Nothing but Spoons* (1969). Am at present poetry editor of *Canadian Forum.* Now working as co-editor of an anthology of writing from the first fifty years of *Canadian Forum* and writing a book on the poetry of Dorothy Livesay.

W. W. E. Ross

Disturbed at chess
thickset square
settled into pain
in his chair
ready to talk
in the smoke-drift
around the bulk
of his head stranded
with hair
creased face firm
above flap of neck
talking
about stress
where it falls
floats
hanging
in grey smoke
sitting
tucked up hunched
flicking
through copybooks
full of poems
made
in his own hand
accounts in small
green ledgers
balanced
with light yet strong
finality of chess
words mated fixed
chessmen at attention
books neat on shelves
painting over the mantel
hard-lined clean
words
moving in blue
smoke through the clutter

around the thickset man
settled with pain
but solid
              in clean
                  hard lines.

Coming Back

A horse framed
in the train window
ambles past a tilting shack.

A car stops
soundless at the crossing
driver and passenger faceless.

One man alone
swathes
sun staring at eye level—

Caught between pole-blinks
and the swoop of wire
this twilight land.

Grain lies dead
in swept curves
arrowheads and cubes.

The sunflowers' Cyclops eyes
wilt heavily on tall stalks;
water towers stretch up.

Square-bodied billboards
stand stiff-legged
above the cars on endless roads.

We feel safe tracked
across land behind glass
till the schedule breaks down.

A train is trapped ahead
and we brake down
beside a silver elevator.

Darkness locks us in the land
empty but for us
coming back behind glass.

And any moment
board buffaloes
might stampede across fields

Where sunflowers rise
throw back feathered heads
and prance around the still train.

Under black night
lines disappear to a point:
we are trapped

While friends and families huddle
where talk echoes to shouts
in bare but gaudy halls

Lights throwing giant
shadows waiting
at the journey's end.

From Yunnan Province 1917

Clogged
in a slither of wet-red clay
here we—mules, coolies
mosquitoes stinging—are
in China
in a deep-sided boat
swirling
across the River Mekong
turbulent as a civil war.
And all for poppies!
Poppies for opium,
And we're supposed to root them/it out.

The Anti-Opium League thinks
quote
drugs make
a moral man a criminal
a healthy man a skeleton
unquote.

Clogged
with conniving officials
indolent coolies
we see
no poppies —
rancour blossoms,
not poppies.
The magistrates grumble,
their province is clear.
Benign Oriental innocence
smiles from their faces.
Sometimes there are a few poppies
and their soldiers tear them out
with great flourishes
while the villagers watch
cringing—
why don't they grow rice?

And so
we go on
by foot and mule and chair
camping in inferior temples
or in tents
looking for poppies
in fields
in the pine forests
shaken
by the screams of peacocks and parrots.

Here
in Yunnan
it's mostly dry scrub
and shrivelled villagers.
Lord Curzon complained
when he visited the trenches
(but now he's back
at his comfortable desk
at the Foreign Office)
he never knew the lower orders
had such white skins.
Here
in Yunnan
they have
dirty yellow bodies
broken
by the thin soil
where nothing grows
except goitres
on the necks of the women.

Then the rain
and fever
malaria
coolies falling sick
all the time.
And we plod on
looking for poppies

but we find   no poppies
so
    make this report
                    quote
Yunnan is sparsely inhabited
by a poor type of native.
Its possibilities
as a poppy-growing district
are conspicuously small.
We have met with nothing
but courtesy and consideration
at the hands of the military
and civil governors.
                    unquote.

Born 1925 in Toronto. Schooling mostly in St. Thomas, Ont. University of Toronto. Married to James Reaney, two children. The only book is the little one published by Alphabet Press, *Lozenges, Poems in the Shapes of Things* and that was done for Christmas, 1965.

Colleen Thibaudeau

As if in code . . .

It's worse over the mountains.
Jettison this and that
dance round the fires till dawn
throws a light lasso
and draws the flatlands in;
Jettison this and that
till point grows into dash
and we get pushed on
by the biggest star in the world.

Unmapped the Blue Mountains.

But everyone goes over anyway
way up and over into that long passage
of no colour but cold, looking back
at the crazed fires blazing on the plains:
chuckle of longlugged books, carvings,
  embroidery,
fires make the past a garden of glads;
roar of dishes, tablecloths, chain bracelets
getting gay as mountain lions or cougars;
swish of baptismal bonnets and winding-sheets
flick round the site like brookfish;
". . . one day see I just happened to be going
  along Piccadilly St . . ."
". . . once I saw I forget but it was light . . ."
fast and free all things with wings.

Fire out. All fires nearly out now.
Seawinds smooth the hands that are crags now
Vineleaves bud on the rawhide circling the brow.

Born in 1935 in New York City. Teach at the University of Manitoba, where I co-edit *The Far Point*. Poems forthcoming or recently published in *Prism*, *Massachusetts Review*, *Poetry Northwest*, *Michigan Quarterly Review*, *Literary Review*.

Myron Turner

December, 1966

for George and Twink Amabile

Sparrows worship at altars of horizon—
their habit is the sun,
pecking dry leaves against the snow;

what half burns a leaf
brown as paper saved
from the gray ease of ash?

like you, delivered,
cut from the green
layer of life

keeping the wooden centre
that clean colour of flesh,
wet enough

for tears—
the smell of gas,
throb of the chain-saw

pressing, drifting,
such innocence of snow
against a door

you cannot open—
this cold, charred,
fire dead, lit

somewhere in the daytime
by the useless sun.
This is a weather

for freezing to fossil
even the wet smell
of new-cut wood,

where nothing
not even the body burns
through to its end

gentle ashes of
exhaustion.

Snowman

Like the first fallen man this snowman resists
perfection: remarkable pectorals bulge
to an apex between his navel and his hip
still I pressed grey glassy buttons from an old coat
down the middle of his ideal existence

with a maroon and yellow tasselled woollen scarf
healed the exposed joint of collarbone and chin
then punched into his eyes four-inch blue triangles
filched plastic shapes
And then I watched him watch me

with his triangular white pupils
they glittered with blindness in the sun;
I walked around behind him like a dog
wary, sniffing, looking for a palm to rub its snout.
Now outside the window, highlighted by the
moon,

he stands on the ball of his feet
as though perched on top of the world
tuberous, like a potato
that has outgrown its polar Eden.
He stares at the night sky around him

mirror scratched to the black paint beneath.
Can he see his face in the specks of silver that
remain
or only a shape like the glassy shadow
standing between us in the windowpane?
Eight below and a high wind.

Will the wind topple him? or some boys?
and into what haphazard pattern (perhaps
the maroon and yellow muffler spreading its
tassels like stars
around the angles of his eyes)?
Or will he shrivel toward spring like some
forgotten fruit?

Born in Winnipeg. Studied at Toronto and Pennsylvania. Teaches English at York. Recently returned from a year of travel and writing in Europe. Five books of verse: *Green World* (1945), *The Second Silence* (1955), *The Season's Lovers* (1958), *The Glass Trumpet* (1966) and *Say Yes* (1969).

Miriam Waddington

Song for Sleeping People

Did you know
America is tilted
like a saucer   on
one side is Persia
on the other is
the moon and
America see-saws
between the two
and in the saucer
swim a million
coloured beads   and
butterflies slice
through the painted
flowers   and children
run around the rim
of the saucer and
pick packets of
flower seeds   blue
forget-me-nots
to throw at the
moon and I step
very light on the
rim of the saucer
I don't want to
make a noise   crack
the surface or
break anything
and I don't want
to wake up the
sleeping people
because one of them
might be me.

All on an Easter Morning

The Thames is choked with daffodils
and Abraham's bridge is falling down,
from Golders Green to Whitechapel
the music of the festivals
drowns in traffic   stars and bells
red rover red rover we call you all over
while the desert bleeds into the sea
and the little white lambs of Passover
skip startled over Hampstead Heath
where Judah's lion is tumbling down
and a wounded world is limping home
from the cold Red River to Galilee
all on an Easter morning.

Anxious

anxious
of course I'm anxious
afraid
of course I'm afraid
I don't know what about
I don't know what of
but I'm afraid
and I feel it's
right to be.

The Carnival Cantata

I was born in Montreal in 1949, but for the last four years I have lived in New York where I attend CCNY when it is neither in a state of siege nor in full-scale revolution. I also work at the Gotham Book Mart. My first book, *The Carnival Cantata*, will be published in 1970. I expect to return to Montreal after graduation.

Henry Weinfield

The merry-go-round
   because there is
a doll's broken head,
And that is what the image is.

The little mimist with the hands,
And the boisterous tragedian
   are
vying for position
   though
she is dead
   no
always dying.

Is that why
            the women are wailing?
Is that why
            the organ is?

And the former is a "masochist,"
And the latter is a "greybeard loon,"
Though they both disappear

Into the prayers of the night,
And the song may survive
as a poignant parody,
Sung for the grammar of it,
the mathematick.

The merry-go-round
   because there is.

Passacaglia

after François Couperin

The march through the woods is a grand
passacaglia
For the huntsman, the stag, and the solemn
crusader.
Do you think the march is long?
The march is long, smiled the sky, and a grief-
wizened tree
Smiled, but the march is short
For the black-eyed faun and his charming mother.

May an arrow pierce her elegant neck,
Noble lords and ladies.
Who will bear homeward the radiant prize,
Grave and ponderous crusaders?
What spoils will you steal
from the sky?
And what is this lust
to be real?
Do you understand my laughter?

For the huntsman, the stag, the *solemn* crusader
The march through the woods is a grand
passacaglia.

Now 43, single, celibate. A clerk, was born in NB, grew up in TO, spent 2 years in BC. Published in *Poets '56*, *Canadian Forum*. Current projects: long poems on Bolshoi Ballet and Toronto Islands. Smoke, don't drink, rarely swear. Naturally curly hair but not really handsome.

George Whipple

From the Japanese

The spring.
And the limestone phallus
Stored for centuries by the housekeeper's
House breaks from its skin of snow.
The virgin spring
Widens to exclude no god.
An ancient need huddles in the bushes.

A stream,
Discovered in the crevices of rocks
Milleniums ago, leaves a mountain
Lifts breasts a half acre
To a kissing sky disrobes the stars.
The sunlight blades the grass in the valleys.

The green aroma of a lake
—Amazing musk—beyond the ashtray
Windows of my eyes, invades the streets.
Spring opens the stone fingers of the city.

And the ice left on the shoulders
Of the rocks melts into the softened trees.
The air floats with flutes—echolalia
Of winds within the poplars.
One hears the newborn cricket in the grass.

Born 1938.
Teaches in the
Creative Writing
Department, UBC.
Poetry editor,
Prism. Co-editor,
*Contemporary
Literature in
Translation*.
Editorial board,
Mundus Artium.
Poetry, fiction,
translations
in many
periodicals. Radio
dramas broadcast
over CBC.

**J. Michael
Yates**

The Great Bear Lake Meditations

MEDITATION 19

I dream cautiously, as if
between high peaks heavy with avalanches.
Seventy-seven days a year
the ice concedes small craft upon
the waters here.
Call it ratio of animal to angel.
Beneath their infinite sky of
ice, the fish dream a slow sound
of breaking.
When passage hardens between banks,
and numbers speak for seconds and years:
cautiously, in my underwater light,
I dream the fish.

MEDITATION 22

The wolves say to the dogs
what the madman of me says
to the citizen.
I need to go fishing until
I need to return.

MEDITATION 23

I watched the bear too long—
until my face became that of a bear
watching a man.
It happened with the salmon
as well: my lower jaw grew into a
great hook, a hump rose on my back,
I reddened until I look like fire under
the water on my way upstream.

I'm waiting at the stream-side,
claw under the current.
Around rocks, through the shallows,
back out of the water, I'll be there,
because there is nothing to do
but arrive.

MEDITATION 24

The salmon circle a spawn,
crimson in clear emerald.
There is a time not to eat
anymore. To go against the current
until death swims beside you tirelessly.
There is a time for the great bear
who waits at the turn of the water
to take the body and all its possible
generations in a single sweep.
But to go aground on the shallows,
side up, not living and not dead, to oil
the air with rot . . . with every orbit around
perpetuity, a little more flesh falls away.

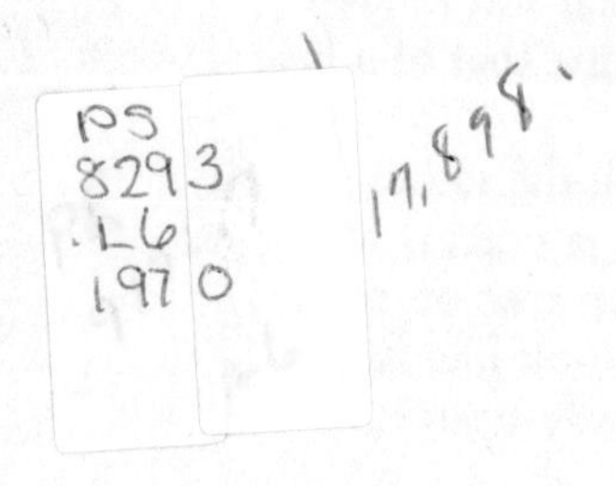

Robert Zend

Reborn in 1956 when, after the Hungarian revolution, he came to Canada. Back home he worked as a film-man and freelance journalist, writer, literary translator and underground poet. He earned his BA in Budapest (1953); his MA in Toronto (1969). Associated with the CBC since 1958. Writes all sorts of poetry: Hungarian and English, metric and free, sad and funny, long and short, good and bad. In 1969 he received a grant from the Canadian Film Development Corporation to produce a film, and a scholarship

Pencil

Someone uses me for writing
his fingers clutch my waist
he holds me tight and leads me on
and holds me tight again

The poem finished he drops me
and I feel diminished
with some surprise I read
the part of me he has worn away

Growth

at first I was a dot but I
  walked and walked and walked

then I became a line but I
  grew and grew and grew

then I became a curve but I
  rose and rose and rose

then I became a spiral but I
  circled and circled and circled

then I became a sphere but I
  swelled and swelled and swelled

then a giant came upon me
  and held me in his hand

what a lovely little dot he said
  I do hope you understand

from the Italian Government to study in Italy. In one of his previous lives—as he faintly recalls—he was a jester. In his present life he tries to stop being one, with no success.

The Little Rat

The little rat races around,
  sniffing about,
  his noticeable nose
  twitching a bit,
and disappears behind a glass partition
where he yanks out someone's file
  to gnaw into it.

Squatting in front of a mirror he admires
  his tiny moustache,
  all the while ruminating:
"I'm an important fellow." His stench
forces others to keep their distance.

Some older mice remember him
when he was a mouse too,
a mouse who squeaked a lot
when there were cats around.
  Now they gather round him,
  and he smiles slyly,
  turning over in his head
  how good they will taste
  when he turns into a cat.